One Left Handed Hug

by

Martin A. Hoeger

authorHOUSE®

AuthorHouse™
1663 Liberty Drive, Suite 200
Bloomington, IN 47403
www.authorhouse.com
Phone: 1-800-839-8640

First published by AuthorHouse 3/11/2009

ISBN: 978-1-4389-4821-8 (sc)

Printed in the United States of America
Bloomington, Indiana

This book is printed on acid-free paper.

This story is dedicated to my family:

My son Jack, without your hard fought determination there would be no story to tell. You have taught me more about life that I could ever dream to teach you.

My son Ben, you have been the rock of our family. You have been asked to grow up beyond your years and have done more for your mother and me than you will ever know.

My daughter Ella, we have missed some important parts of your early years and promise to make up for it in years to come.

My siblings, the Hoeger clan and Green family, we were always taught that friends are nice but family is forever. You have been there for Jen and me for so much we could never thank you enough.

Tom and Sis Oeschger, thank you for all of your support and help in fighting Jacks illness. You listened to us on the hard days and were able to give us a smile when it felt almost impossible to smile.

Rosemary and Dan Hoeger, mom and dad what can be said other than thank you. You gave my children a place to call home while we could not be there. You drove them to us whenever we asked so that we could see them. Most of all you taught me what I could only hope to be as a parent.

My wife Jen, you promised to be true to me for better, for worse, for richer, for poor, in sickness and in health and for some reason in our 12 years of marriage we have been tested in everyone. I married my best friend 12 years ago and thank god for you every day. I love you.

Foreward

One left-handed hug
Cynthia Wetmore, M.D., Ph. D

I first met Jackson Hoeger and his family in May 2005. We connected at first meeting. His eyes were guarded as he peered at me in the exam room. He was curled up in his mother's lap. He seemed engaged in his surroundings but so tired and scared, as were his parents Jen and Marty. My thoughts were caught up in how to put them at ease and also, in how to help Jack battle this tumor while still preserving his sense of self. In medicine, as in parenting, we are not to have favorites. As a physician at Mayo Clinic, the model of care is to strive for the best every patient, every time. The patient always comes first. The science of medicine is to find cures to stop the tumor cells from dividing and spreading throughout the body. The art of medicine is to cradle the young person and family in love and compassion, to help them to understand what lies ahead and feel that they have a partner at every step of the way. I feel blessed and privileged to be able to care for children and their families as they battle brain cancer and have great joy as I have been invited by Jack's parents to contribute to their story.

Brain tumors are the most common solid tumor of childhood, only leukemia is more common as a type of cancer in children. As I explain to my patient families, most pediatric cancers arise as a kind of "typo" or in cell's DNA as it is copied and segregated into the two daughter cells. Such "typos" occur in thousands of cells everyday in each of our bodies but most of those errors do not result in a growth advantage and those cells do not survive. In some cases, the "typo" or mutation occurs in a gene that gives the cell a growth advantage and the cells loose their normal regulation of control over cell proliferation and death. These are the cells that grow into a tumor. Presently, we do not know of the major genes involved in promoting tumor growth. We have some ideas about a few genes that are mutated in a small proportion of pediatric brain tumors but most of the pathways in the molecular regulation of brain tumor growth are not yet known.

One of the greatest challenges in treating brain tumors in children and adolescents is the fact that their nervous system is still developing through the first decade of life. Usually therapy consists of surgical resection of as much of the tumor as possible, then several months of chemotherapy and/or radiation therapy to try to kill the tumor cells. In Jack's case, this was a particular challenge because while his tumor was one of the most common families of brain tumor (primitive neuroectodermal tumor or PNET) is was extremely unusual in that there was no primary lesion that could be removed surgically. Rather, Jack's tumor formed a type of "frosting" coating the surfaces of his brain and spine. These tumor cells were irritating normal brain cells and causing seizures. Generally, this type of tumor in this area of the brain is difficult to treat and patients have less than 20% chance of survival. Part of the struggle in Jack's care was to target therapy to the tumor cells while still hoping to preserve as much normal function of his brain as possible. At this time it is impossible to selectively kill tumor cells without also harming the normal cells of the developing brain. I hope that one day, we will be able to understand more about the genes and pathways that initiate and promote brain tumor growth so that we may be able to selectively target tumor cells and leave the remaining normal cells unharmed. This is the goal that I and many others have committed our lives to attaining.

I marvel at Jack's recovery. He has been tumor free for more than two years now. He has emerged from the seizures, malnutrition, infections and low blood counts with a new sparkle in his eyes. Jack is back to playing baseball and being a little boy, wrestling with his brother and sister and living each day to the fullest. He is speaking out and telling his story. Jen and Marty asked me what they could do to help other children with cancer and I told them to use their words and tell Jack's remarkable story. I hope that those who read Jack's story take from it his hope and inspiration. While medicine is becoming ever more technical, it is still an art and we do not have all of the answers. In Jack's honor may we all LiveStrong and continue to fight for a cure to cancer.

Peace.

ACKNOWLEDGMENTS

This story of Jack would not be possible with out the help of several people.

Rose Kramer, you were the first to know about this little project and gave me the courage to proceed. Your help with the book was invaluable and is the reason this project has become a reality.

Steve Lounsberry, you gave me confidence to pursue this project. Our early morning coffee sessions I will never forget.

Steve and Christy Koronczok, your dedication to children's fight against cancer has made me realize the importance of sharing this story with others to show that the fight can be won.

Stacey Hodges, the cover says it all. This photo has been admired by many people, you have a true gift.

Bryce Parks, the producer of the "Livestrong Jack" video. Your video has produced more than 50,000 hits on youtube but you have produced more than a video, you gave me the inspiration to share more of Jacks story.

To everyone who have logged on to Jacks caringbridge web page. All 165,000 of you. We hope you enjoy this project.

"Hope is the thing with feathers
That perches in the soul,
And sings the tune—without the words,
And never stops at all."
- Emily Dickinson

Chapter 1
A Mother's Intuition

Jackson is my seven-year-old son. My wife Jen gave birth to Jackson Thomas Hoeger on June 27, 1999. We had been married for three years, both 27 years old, and living the American dream. We had good jobs, we just moved into our first brand new home in a great neighborhood and now we were about to take home a healthy baby boy.

From an early age, as Jack was learning to crawl, walk, and then run, he was a very coordinated kid. At many of his doctor's appointments his pediatrician would ask, "What sport will Jack be participating in? He is so coordinated for his age. His potential is endless." I am sure that is what doctors say to all new parents, but just the same I always thought he would be something special.

Over the next five years our family grew to five as two more wonderful children joined Jack—Ben and Ella. Jack was the "big brother" and loved to play the role, helping out with anything and everything—whether we needed it or not!

In the fall of 2004, at age 5, Jack entered pre-kindergarten. Jen and I went to his school on different occasions, such as conferences and classroom parties, and we were so proud of how he was developing his fine motor skills—but more importantly we were encouraged that his social skills seemed to be developing as well. Jack was probably ready for kindergarten since he had already spent two years at pre-school, but we decided because he was pretty small for his age it would be better to send him to Alternative Kindergarten for one year before sending him on to kindergarten.

November 2004

Jack woke up one morning in the late fall with a headache followed by vomiting and then he fell asleep for several hours. At first we thought the flu had paid a visit to our house or that it was some type of virus. After a day of this we took Jack to the doctor's office. Our suspicions were correct, the doctor said that he may have picked up a virus at school and he also had an ear infection—something most parents hear several times a year when you have young children.

The headaches and vomiting would come and go for the next week and Jen was starting to become very worried. I will say that a mother's intuition should never be disregarded. I left home early on a Saturday morning to go to an Iowa football game with some friends and Jen called to say that after running some tests at the doctor's office, the test showed that Jack had strep. We were relieved that we finally had something to treat.

The next week we received a call from Jack's teacher asking us to come in for a visit to discuss Jack's progress in school. With Jack being our first child in school we thought this was a normal meeting. When we got there we went through his work binder to see that his work was above normal at the beginning of the year and now in early November it had deteriorated to the point that he was writing his name backwards, coloring outside the lines, and not cutting like he was capable of doing. She proceeded to ask if everything was OK at home or if we had noticed anything different in Jack. We were puzzled and confused—and then the mother's intuition set in again telling Jen that there was more to Jack's illness than what we had thought.

With Jack weighing heavily on my mind, I woke up at 3:00 a.m. with a sudden inspiration. To my surprise, Jen was wide awake as well. I said, "Tomorrow I am going to take Jack to the eye doctor." My thought was that Jack had never been given an eye exam and it only made sense that his headaches might be because this kid can't see. During the eye exam Jack was great and so excited at the idea that he might be getting glasses. After some tests Dr. Kara came in with an assistant and asked that Jack go with the assistant to the treasure chest to get his prize. She then told me that the photos of Jack eyes had shown that he had papillodema, which is a buildup of pressure behind

11

the eyes. She suggested that we take the results to the pediatrician and get a CT scan as soon as possible.

As I was on the way to the doctor's office that afternoon to go over the test results, I was trying not to let the worst of thoughts enter my mind, but then you think that you want to be prepared for the news that may come. The doctor went over the results with me and went on to tell me that Jack did not have papilledema and that Dr. Kara, while being a good eye doctor, may have misread the photos, therefore becoming too anxious about the CT. He then said that if we wanted him to schedule the CT to put our minds at ease he would schedule a CT. We asked him to schedule it and we would finally know what was going on.

That afternoon Dr. Kara called to see how we did at the doctor's office. I shared with her that the CT was being scheduled and that the pediatrician had differed from her opinion in regard to her papilledema diagnosis and that they would be doing the scan in three weeks. She responded by saying that was unacceptable and she would call me back. At 9:45 p.m. she called and asked if we could have Jack to the hospital at 7:30 the next morning for the CT. We were beside ourselves with this turn of events. I asked her what had changed. She shared with me that her neighbor is a radiologist and she called in a favor.

The next morning at the hospital we were in the waiting room while Jack was getting tested. Jen and my mom were sitting on one side of the room talking small talk trying not to think about anything bad. I was pacing back and forth thinking to myself, "There is nothing wrong with Jack. Everything is going to be normal." I remember that there was an older lady in the room, sitting in a wheelchair talking to whoever would talk to her. Since Jen and my mom were on the other side of the room talking, that left me. She was very persistent in asking why we were there and when I told her she responded by telling me the she had lost a son once and that she would pray for me. A sense of anger came over me that she had said this because we were not going to lose a son and everything was going to be fine!

The doctor came into the waiting room and announced that everything looked great and Jack could go home. Jen and my mom began to cry and the old lady in the wheelchair yelled out, "Praise the Lord!" as loud as she could! I was standing there thinking, "Let's get the hell out of here and take our boy home!"

That night Jen and I had the best night's sleep for weeks and little did we know it was the best night's sleep we'd have for over a year to come.

Chapter 2
The Fight Begins

December 2004

After work one evening, Jack and his buddy Jake and I were going to go to Cedar Falls to watch the University of Iowa wrestle the University of Northern Iowa. Around 4:00 p.m. Jake's mom, Jenny, who was also our daycare provider and a good childhood friend of Jen's, called to say that Jack was acting "different" and that she was worried about him. As chance would have it, I was close by and went to get Jack right away. When I got there, Jack had a glossy look on his face but was able to walk and talk. He said that his leg was falling asleep and he felt funny. I took him to the emergency room and called Jen on the way. As you can imagine, Jen began to panic and wondered what was going on. I tried my best to calm her down and really downplayed my concerns as to what was happening to Jack. Jen works as a speech therapist in a small-town hospital about 45 minutes away from our home. I was concerned for Jack, but also wanted to make sure that in a sense of urgency Jen didn't try to make it to the hospital in record time and get in an accident herself.

I had Jack walk into the hospital while holding my hand so that I could see how he was doing. He started to drag his left foot as he stepped. When we got there we did the normal ER check-in. They took his vitals, asked a hundred questions, and then asked us to wait. I remember looking around at the empty waiting room. I kept talking to Jack and his speech became worse as time went on. He was speaking with a slight slur. They finally came to get us and when the ER doc came in I was talking a mile a minute trying to relate what was happening. He slowed me down and assured me that everything looked OK and that he was going to run some tests. He watched Jack walk two steps and said, "Looks good." Jack was walking now with a slight drag to his left leg. I said, "He does not walk that way!" The doctor then asked me to let him finish. He asked if Jack had gotten into anything at the daycare, like alcohol or cleaning supplies. I remember thinking, "Of course! It has to be something like that!" I called Jenny, the daycare provider, and she assured me that this was not the case. By now Jen had arrived and was what I would call in a "controlled panic." She wanted to become educated on what was going on as soon as possible, but yet wanted to scream her emotions throughout the hospital. The ER doctor was in and out of the room asking different questions. Jen finally looked at him and said, "If you don't know what to do, then transfer us to the U." The "U" is the University of Iowa Hospitals, which is located 20 minutes away and is a world renowned hospital in many specialty areas.

As you can imagine, the doctor was not overly thrilled to hear those words. He told us not to overreact and that they were going to "run some more tests." I stated that he had said that an hour ago and nothing had happened! Nothing is more frustrating than sitting in an ER room knowing that they are not overly busy and that you are made to wait.

My parents (who also live in Cedar Rapids) had now arrived to get an update on how Jack was doing. Jen had called them to pick up Ben and Ella from daycare. They opted to come to the hospital instead and have my sister pick up the two kids. At first I was kind of pissed because I felt that until we knew what was going on we didn't need a ton of people showing up. But I was also secretly relieved to have them there.

One of the things the doctor had requested was that we try to get Jack to eat. The nurse brought in some chocolate pudding. She tried to feed him the pudding and it just sat on his lips, by this time he couldn't open his mouth. He then stared off to the right and started having convulsions and all hell broke loose. I was yelling for the doctor and Jen was balled up in the corner of the room crying, thinking she was losing her son. I asked my dad to pick her up and get her out of the room. I had Jack in my arms and somehow calmly talked to him, asking him to hang in there and to wake up, and that Daddy loves him. It was such a lonely feeling to look into his eyes and not know if he could see or hear me. Then, looking up at the door, wondering where the doctor was and seeing a nurse standing in the doorway, I yelled, "Go get the God damn doctor!" Much to my surprise the doctor was standing right across from me watching what was going on. I said, "Will you please do something?" They gave Jack a shot of Valium that basically knocked him out. By this time they had Jack hooked up to the monitors and wires that you see on a TV show—but this was very real. With all of the beeps in the background we all were sitting there in disbelief. The doctor returned to the room telling us that they were going to transfer him to the U as soon as possible and only one of us was going to be able to ride in the ambulance.

I rode in the ambulance while Jen went with my parents. Now I was very relieved that my parents had come to the hospital. Remember when I said that the U was twenty minutes from where we lived? Well in the ambulance it was around eight minutes of drive time. Much to my surprise, when we pulled up, my mom, dad, and Jen were already there! (I think my dad may have broken a few of Iowa's "rules of the road!") The next 12 hours were full of blood tests and questions about his history. They preformed a spinal tap and an MRI. All of the results came back showing that Jack was normal.

The next morning Jack woke up like nothing had happened and asked right away, "Can I have some pancakes?" Jen and I looked at each other like, "What the hell is going on?" The neurologist came in and said that they wanted to run some more tests and that everything to this point looked like Jack was suffering from "chronic migraine" headaches. She explained that they can get so bad that they will make a person appear to have a "TIA" otherwise known as a Transient Ischemic Attack, or minor stroke. Jack had lost some motion on his left side, which was going to take some time to recover and he would need some therapy to rebuild his strength but he should be back to normal in no time.

The next couple of days were spent in the hospital for observation and for Jack to regain his strength that he had lost in his left side. When we met with the neurologist I brought up the issue of Jack's eye appointment and the papillodema. She indicated that the there were no signs of that but if we wanted her to she would refer us to an ophthalmologist at the U. We asked for the appointment to be scheduled as soon as possible.

Chapter 3
A Rare Form

Our appointment with the ophthalmologist was a quick one. We were in the room with him maybe two minutes. He looked into Jack's eyes and said, "I will be right back." Five minutes later he came back and said that Jack had what was called papillodema and he wanted to have someone else look at him. There's that word again—papillodema—what was the eye doctor able to see that the regular doctors could not? I was confused at this discovery, but not surprised.

Then, what was about to happen next may have saved our son's life. We met Dr. Lee, a neuro-ophthalmologist, who had agreed to see us immediately. During our appointment he stated that Dr. Kara was right all along and that he did not agree with the chronic migraine diagnosis. I asked him why every **eye** doctor was able to see the papillodema but the other doctors were not able to. Dr. Lee explained to me that the regular doctors were looking into the eye with a regular household flashlight and that the eye doctors were using a laser beam. The other doctors were simply not looking for papillodema. He ran a series of tests on Jack over the next couple of days and finally came up with a diagnosis of Pseudotumor cerrebri, a fluid buildup around the brain that is common in middle-aged overweight woman. Jack was a very rare case, with only a couple of other kids known to have it. During our appointment Dr. Lee shared with us that when Jack had been admitted to the hospital and they performed a spinal tap on him they did not measure the spinal fluid pressure and that it would have helped with this diagnosis. We left there with a prescription for Diamox (which is a water-based pill to dilute the liquid around his brain) and scheduled appointments with Dr. Lee every week for the next month so he could monitor Jack.

With every appointment Dr. Lee saw improvement. The fluid was going away and by month's end he scheduled us six weeks out for a follow-up appointment.

Jack went back to school and we were living like a normal family. March arrived and our follow-up appointments with Dr. Lee and the neurologist that had seen Jack when he was admitted. It looked like the worst was behind us. At our last appointment with the neurologist she apologized for all that we had gone through and that she was also sorry for the misdiagnosis. We left that appointment feeling that as long as Jack was cured we had no qualms about who was right and who was wrong. That is why they call it "practicing medicine" right?

On a bright sunny Saturday morning I was off to work for a couple of hours. Jen arranged for Jack to have a play date over and as they were doing crafts at the table Jen noticed that Jack was staring off for a couple of seconds. She then noticed that he was sitting at the table perfectly still staring off to the left with no emotion. She moved him to the couch and yelled for the neighbor to help. After a minute of this our neighbor, Denny, drove Jen and Jack to the hospital. She called me on the way; my office is only two blocks away from the hospital. I arrived at the ER before they arrived and told the ER people that we were not going to register and to get the ambulance ready. We were going to Iowa City. They looked at me like I was crazy. I said, "Pull up his history and you will see." She pulled it up and within minutes of Jack showing up the paramedics were ready to go.

When we arrived in Iowa City this time we were told that the neurologist that had seen Jack the first time was on leave and that we would be seeing another doctor and that he was a really good doctor who specializes in epilepsy. As soon as those words came out of the nurse's mouth I felt uneasy. I told Jen that if that doctor walks in the room diagnosing Jack with epilepsy then we were going to get another opinion. We met with the doctor, he did another CT, and again everything looked normal.

The next morning the doctor came to our room stating that it was his belief that Jack did not have Pseudotumor cerrebri. He recommended putting Jack on seizure medicine to control his epilepsy. We asked to

23

meet with Dr. Lee first before we did anything. As always, Dr. Lee agreed to see us immediately.

In our meeting with Dr. Lee he agreed that Jack did not have Pseudotumor cerrebri. He also said that he felt Jack did not have epilepsy either. It was his feeling that Jack had something very serious going on with him and he wanted to become aggressive in finding out what it was. He suggested that we do a series of tests that included a spinal tap and this time he would measure the pressure, as well as doing a Magnetic Resonance Imaging (MRI) and a Magnetic Resonance Aniogram (MRA). The MRI is a test that is used to find problems such as tumors, bleeding, blood vessel problems, or infection. The MRA is a type of MRI that can find problems with the blood vessels that may be causing reduced blood flow. With MRA technology, both the blood flow and the condition of the blood vessel walls can be seen. Although the tests would require sedation, which posed some risk for a small child, he felt it would help in finding out what was going on with Jack. We agreed. We were ready for any news, good or bad. We just wanted to find out what was going on with our little boy. When we returned to our room the nurse was there waiting for us with our discharge papers. We informed her that we were staying for further tests ordered by Dr. Lee. The nurse left to get the doctor to speak with us. The doctor came in to explain that he was Jack's primary physician and that Dr. Lee was considered a consultant and that since he did not agree with Dr. Lee's plan he therefore cancelled the entire series of test that had been ordered. He informed us that the sedation was not worth the risk and he thought he had the correct diagnosis. We looked at him in disbelief and asked that he refer us to the Mayo Clinic in Rochester, Minnesota. He told us that he welcomed a second opinion, but would not refer us and that we could do it ourselves over the Internet.

I often wonder if doctors ever think about the way that they affect patients, or in this case, parents of the patient, when they talk to them? Right now I felt that we had a doctor that was not willing to help us find a cure for Jack. He was making it hard on us to even get a second opinion! At that time I mentally said to myself that if he was wrong that I would make sure that he would know about it. What I don't think he understood was that we were not on a mission to prove him wrong. The fact was that I was hoping he was right. My hope was that we would go to Mayo, they would tell us that the doctors at the U of I were right, and that Jack had epilepsy. Instead, he treated us like we were using our son like a medical research project and that it was all unnecessary.

We left the hospital with a prescription for a medicine, an emergency dose of Diastat. Diastat is quick-dose medicine that when administered rectally would bring Jack out of a seizure in the event that it lasted longer than five minutes.

We also left the hospital with an overwhelming despair as to how we were going to get Jack to the Mayo Clinic. To us, the Mayo Clinic was this huge institution and how could we ever get them to take us in? We called our pediatrician to see if he could be of some help. He informed us that he did not have any connections at the Mayo Clinic and we should try ourselves. Jen got on the computer on a mission to research Mayo. She was persistent to the point that she finally got through to the neurology department to talk to them about Jack's case. They got us on the schedule for the first of May— almost six weeks away.

The next day I took Jack to a therapy appointment. During that session Jack suffered three seizures in a fifteen-minute period. Each one had me looking at the clock getting the Diastat ready to give to him if it were to go one second past five minutes. I called Jen and let her know about the seizures and she persuaded me, or more or less insisted, that I call the pediatrician and have him contact the neurologist at Mayo to see if they could get us in sooner. I was reluctant at first because who am I to tell a doctor what to do? I called him anyway to inform him of Jack's status. His response was he didn't think it would do any good for him to call them. With a sense of urgency in my voice I said, "Gary we are to see a Dr. Kotagal and here is the 1-800 number. You tell them that I will be leaving here at 3:00 p.m. today and will be in their waiting room tomorrow morning at 8:00 a.m. and I will stay there until they see my son." He said he understood and would do whatever he could to help. Within a half hour Mayo Clinic called me to inform me that we had an appointment with Dr. Kotagal at 3:00 p.m. the next day.

That night we took Ben and Ella over to my parent's house. While we were walking out the door Ben walked over to Jack and gave him a hug. Was that a sign? Would it be the last one for the two brothers?

Chapter 4
Our Journey Begins

Late March 2005

So there we were, driving three hours north on a two-lane highway to an unfamiliar place with an uncertain future. Small talk wouldn't fill the void and we were all "talked out" concerning Jack's illness and guessing what could be wrong. We arrived in Rochester around 11:00 p.m. that evening and checked into a hotel. After the normal commotion of checking into a hotel had been done I was so anxious for that night to be over and start the next day. I felt like we were losing what could be valuable time and the sooner we got to talk to the doctors the sooner we would find out what was wrong with Jack.

As soon as we were settled into the room I saw that I had missed some phone calls on my cell. I had a message from my boss, Duane, who I greatly admire and respect. His message was this, "Marty I understand that you and Jen are on your way to Rochester with Jack. Please know that everyone at True North is thinking of your family and do not worry about anything back here at the office. Come back only when Jack is healthy." I told Jen about the message and we felt a huge pressure lifted off our shoulders. We were very concerned about how we were going to balance work, family, and Jack while being three hours from home.

The next morning we awoke with a plan. Here we were, about to go to the huge institution of medicine without having any idea of where exactly we were to go. Even though our appointment wasn't until 3:00 p.m., we wanted to go right away to make sure we knew where we were going. We set out around 9:00 a.m. to find East 9 in the Mayo building. We drove three blocks from the hotel and there it was—the Mayo building we were looking for! We had found it in 5 minutes, now what? The weather was nice so we drove around looking for a park. We couldn't find one so we ended up going to an elementary school to let Jack play. It was as if we had forgotten about why we were there, we just enjoyed the time together.

After lunch we decided we had better set off for where East 9 was in the Mayo building. We found it rather quickly, and then sat in the waiting room, anxious, for almost an hour waiting for our name to be called.

"Jackson Hoeger" the nurse called on the intercom. After taking his height and weight we proceeded down a long hallway to the exam room. We sat in there for a couple of minutes while waiting for Dr.

Kotagal. The door opened and it was a lady who introduced herself as a resident and wanted to get Jack's information. We had a backpack full of Jack's medical history along with his Diastat. We ended up naming it the "seizure bag" and it became part of our life since we carried it with us everywhere we went. We went over it quite thoroughly with her while she listened and wrote some notes. She then examined Jack and said, "I will be back." She left the room and a few moments later a man of small stature walked into the room with a gentle feel about him. He shook our hands, smiled, and said, "Hello, I am Dr. Kotagal." He sat down and asked us to give him a brief history as to why we ended up a Mayo. I thought to myself, "Didn't you read the notes from the resident?" As we were going through this I noticed that he was not writing anything down and really concentrating on what we were saying and watching Jack and his movements. He then examined Jack and said, "This is what we are going to do: tomorrow we are going to do an EEG on Jack to check out his brain activity. I want to get his CT scans from the U of I hospitals and go over them. Then we are going to do our own set of scans, which consist of an MRI and spinal tap to compare the two." He then said, "I hope you planned on staying for a couple of days."

As we left the appointment, we sat in the van and looked each other. I said to Jen, "What do you think?" Jen looked at me and said, "I have a good feeling about him and feel that we are on the right path." Even though we didn't have any more knowledge of what was wrong with Jack, we felt we were going to find our answers sooner rather than later.

The next morning we reported to the 4th floor of the Gonda building for his EEG. The process for this test was not a very comfortable one for Jack. They put what looks like a swimmer's cap with several wires sticking out of it on his head then put a needle in each hole to glue it to his scalp. The test lasted around 30 minutes. Then we were off to St. Mary's Hospital, which was located down the road from the Mayo Clinic, for his MRI and spinal tap. For this test Jack had sedation and it would last for a little over an hour.

While waiting with Jen to hear Jack's name called, a lady came up to us in the waiting room and introduced herself as the radiologist assistant. She gave Jack a mask to play with. She explained to him that he would need to breathe in and out of it. He smiled and told her he could do that. The next person who came out was the radiologist. He drew a happy face on a deflated balloon and informed Jack that he could make that balloon dance if he blew into the mask hard enough. Jack smiled and said he could do it. Then the anesthesiologist came out to explain the procedure to us. He looked at Jack and said, "Jack do you like root beer, bubble gum, or watermelon?" Jack said root beer and the doctor rubbed a chemical on the mask and asked Jack to smell it. Jack looked up with a smile and said roooot beeeer! We all laughed and they called Jack's name. Because the room was so small, only one parent was allowed to go back, so I carried Jack back to the room where everyone was waiting. The thing that impressed me was that everyone that was in this room with all this big equipment had already introduced themselves to Jack so everyone was familiar. There was the balloon with the happy face; there was the mask that smelled like root beer. Within seconds Jack was out.

Jen and I were then escorted upstairs to the waiting room. After awhile a nurse who was in the spinal tap procedure came into the waiting room to see us. She informed us that Jack was doing fine. She explained that when they checked the spinal fluid pressure, the pressure was so high they could not measure it and they removed a lot of fluid. She further informed us that we would have an appointment scheduled the next morning with Dr. Kotagal to go over the results.

The next morning, while going over the results with Dr. Kotagal, he informed us that the scan looked fine but he was concerned with the EEG. It looked like Jack was having hundreds of seizures a minute while he was sleeping and sometimes even while he was awake. He also said that when they measured the pressure of his spinal fluid for the spinal tap that it measured off the charts. We asked what that meant and he told us that it was pretty rare and the next time they sedated him for a test he wanted to do another one. So where do we go from here? He suggested that we meet with a neurosurgeon to discuss doing a "brain biopsy." They would drill a small hole about the size of a nickel through Jack's skull to his brain and then put an instrument through the hole and clip a small piece of the brain off to run tests on. He was going to schedule the consultation right away.

While at the hotel that evening we received the message that we were to meet Dr. Raffle, who was the neurosurgeon, the next morning for the consult.

In our meeting with Dr. Raffle he assured us that it was a very common procedure, but wanted to make sure that every other test was performed before they drilled through his skull. He called Dr. Kotagal in and the two of them, in front of us, went over the scans and the spinal tap. He asked if we had consulted with an infectious specialist. We had no idea what he was talking about. He explained to us that this all may be because Jack may have come in contact with a rare fungus or disease that caused his seizures and cognitive changes.

Later that day we met with a doctor who specialized in infectious diseases. We went through a series of questions like: "Has Jack ever gone camping in Wisconsin and touched a bird feather?" Has Jack ever been bitten by a dog in Indiana?" Imagine three pages of those types of questions. Jen was concerned that Jack's illness could have been caused by a swim in the Mississippi River and the doctor said matter-of-factly, "You WANT this to be due to fungus, you can cure that with antibiotics." After that meeting I wasn't sure if Jen was ever going to let our kids go outside again. They took some blood tests and sent them to labs all over the country. We went back to the hotel praying that Jack had a rare CURABLE fungus. How many times do you ever hear a parent say that?

After three days in Rochester we were told to go home for the weekend and return the following week for the blood test results. Going home was bittersweet. We were able to see Ben and Ella and also sleep in our own bed. But you always hear people say, "We went to Mayo and had a diagnosis in a couple of days." We were scared leaving Rochester without answers.

When we returned to Rochester Monday we met with Dr. Kotagal to update him on Jack's seizure status. At this time Jack was only having a couple of break-through seizures a day and most of them lasted only a couple of seconds per incident. Dr. Kotagal put Jack on a second seizure medicine. He informed us that when you add another medication you have to start out at a low dosage and increase it over time and then decrease his other medication over time so as not to shock his system. Without really understanding why one drug works and another one does not, changing medicines would quickly become a way of life for us.

The blood test came back negative and he did not have a rare infection. The talk then went back to performing that brain biopsy. In a phone conversation with Dr. Raffle they came up with the idea of having one more MRI done, along with a MRV and another spinal test. This was going to be scheduled as soon as possible. When we met with the scheduling nurse she informed us it would be three weeks out. Dr. Kotagal overheard her tell us that and he approached the desk and said, "Mr. and Mrs. Hoeger can you wait in the waiting room? I will see what I can do." Ten minutes later he came to the waiting room and said, "How will 9:00 a.m. tomorrow morning work?" We sat there with a blank stare on our faces and said, "Okay." Then Jen asked how he got it moved up? He smiled and said, "The anesthesiologist is my neighbor. She owed me one."

The next morning in the waiting room we met three people who would be very instrumental in our lives for the next year and a half. The nurse came in with a resident and introduced Dr. Andy Hashikawa to us. He looked at us and smiled and said, "Dr. Andy is fine." Dr. Andy examined Jack, then the anesthesiologist came in and he introduced himself as Dr. McKenzie. He was an older man who wore a surgeon's hat that had black and white markings like a cow. He was a jolly man and you knew it just tore him up inside to see a small child suffer. He came in and made a balloon out of a glove and showed Jack how to shoot his dad with water in a dull syringe. He went over the procedure with us, knowing that we had heard it a thousand times by now. He looked at Jack and said, "Who gets to go back with you today?" Jack looked at Dr. Andy and Dr. McKenzie and said, "That's OK I think I will go back by myself." Both doctors looked shocked and so did we!

I remember thinking to myself that when a five year old tells a nurse that if she puts the rubber band **over** his sleeve when they take blood that it doesn't hurt as much, and when he is OK to go with two strange doctors to get sedated, that he has experienced way too much at such a young age. I also remember thinking how brave he is!

Friday May 13, 2005

The next day we met with Dr. Kotagal to go over the test results once again. This time he had news. He explained to us that they found what looked like a "lighting up" of cells on his brain. When they read a scan, black is good and white is bad. Jack had an **entire white scan.** This discovery came about due to the MRV, which was a scan of the ventricles. He said they ran the lab test on the spinal fluid and the results came back showing tumor cells floating in his spinal region and his brain was coated with tumor cells "like frosting on a cake." He told us that for some reason the cancer cells never formed into a mass and that was the reason why it was so hard to find. He told us that he would have to run some more tests to find out what kind of cancer it was, but he wanted to refer us to a good friend and colleague of his, Dr. Cynthia Wetmore, a neuro-oncologist as soon as possible in order to come up with a treatment plan. He had a sense of urgency in his voice. We sat there in disbelief. Our worst fear had come true. The very words we were afraid to hear had been spoken. **JACK HAS CANCER.**

For whatever reason, we never broke down, we just sat there—stunned. Jen asked what the prognosis was. He told us he did not have that answer and encouraged us not to lose hope but he just did not have that answer. He paged Dr. Wetmore to see when she would be able to meet with us. She returned his call immediately, told him it would be a couple of days, and that we should go home for the weekend and plan on seeing her on Tuesday afternoon.

After we left the doctor's office, we headed to the mall food court before heading home. Jack had been very specific about what he wanted to eat and it changed almost daily so we figured out that the food court was generally a fool-proof plan. While Jen was helping Jack with his food, my phone rang. It was my parent's phone number and they were calling for an update. I answered the phone and walked away to a corner booth away from Jen and Jack. My mom was on the line. After some small talk about Ben and Ella, Mom asked if we had any news on Jack yet. I sat there in silence for a moment, then, again, my mom said, "Marty what's going on? Have you heard anything yet?" She then yelled for my dad to get on the other phone. He picked up the phone and said, "What did you find out?" With tears coming down my face, I said in a cracked voice, "Jack has cancer." I remember looking over across the food court at Jen and Jack and tried to pull it together. I need to be strong for them and not be like this. I sat up and said we were coming home that night for the weekend then coming back on Tuesday to meet with the oncologist. We didn't know anything other than *it's cancer* and we didn't know what kind nor what the prognosis would be. They sat in stunned silence on the phone. They told me that they loved us all and they would be there to do whatever we needed.

On our way home that night we tried to discuss everything **but** Jack's illness. Because we were not sure what it was or what the next year of our lives would be like, it was hard to talk about, but we couldn't think about anything else. Finally Jen broke down. Why Jack? Why did this happen to Jack?—all of the questions I was thinking, and anyone would be thinking, but will never know the answers to. When we returned home that evening Jen took Jack inside and I was outside cleaning out the van. Our neighbors, Denny and Mardeen and Lloyd and Deb were outside and came over to our driveway to see what we had found out. I was trying to keep myself busy cleaning the van so I wouldn't have to say those words again. Jen came out to help unload and walked up to Mardeen and Deb and hugged them and started crying. It was so hard to talk about with people because we were not sure what to say. He had cancer but we didn't know anything else. Up to this point we had so much support from all of our friends and family that we couldn't imagine leaning on them any more than we already had. Boy were we wrong!

Throughout that weekend we stayed real low key. We wanted to spend time alone with Ben and Ella and make sure that Jack rested.

He didn't know anything was wrong with him and we were trying to protect him from everything and everyone.

We left the following Monday for Rochester, with again, a week's worth of clothes and the uncertainty of what lay ahead.

Chapter 5
A Year in Hell at a Great Place

While driving up to Rochester I remember thinking how hard it must have been for my parents to say goodbye to Jack, not knowing when they would see him again or **if** they would ever see him again. How hard it was on Jen's parents, Tom and Sis, as well. They are both having their own health problems and are not able to travel like they would like to and have to rely on talking to Jack on the phone. How is this going to affect people? How is a six-year-old boy's illness going to affect people? We had no idea.

Tuesday morning we decided to go to Panera Bread for lunch before we went to meet with Dr. Wetmore. While walking in I held the door for some ladies walking out. The exchange was like you wanted to hold the door for them to be polite but they weren't sure you were holding the door for them so they half walked in and stopped. With my nerves on edge I looked at them like "in or out ladies, let's go." While at the counter, ready to order, Jen and I had a disagreement as what to order. She ordered what she wanted and I ordered what I thought she wanted me to order so we could split it with Jack. When we sat down we found we had both ordered the same thing! Like I said, my nerves were shot and so were Jen's. We had some looks and words back and forth. I finally stood up and said, "I'm leaving. I'll be in the van." Pissed off, I left the restaurant, knocking over a chair as I was leaving. As I reached the van I realized I didn't have the keys—Jen did. So there I stood, embarrassed at my actions, standing in the parking lot where everyone who witnessed me being a jerk could come out and see me locked out of my own car. Can this day get any worse?

Well it could. When we got to the doctor's office, Dr. Wetmore walked in and said hello. She took one look at us and said, "Have I seen you guys before?" Then she said, "I think I saw you at Panera Bread today." My heart just sank. Here we were, seeing this doctor about saving my son's life and she might have just witnessed me acting like a jerk in public!

Dr. Wetmore explained to us that Jack's illness is curable and it was her mission to make sure that he lived a normal happy life. She then laid out his treatment plan. She informed us that Jack's cancer is known as Primitive Neuroectodermal Tumor (PNET). It is not a rare disease but the form that Jack had was extremely rare. Without a tumor mass and it being so diffuse, they would not be able to operate to remove the cancer. So she explained that we had to depend solely on chemotherapy and radiation.

We found ourselves loaded down with an enormous amount of information from the oncologist and radiologists. Jen couldn't even speak during the radiologist consultation. I asked her if she was OK and she told me that she was afraid if she started to talk she would fall apart and start crying. She said she couldn't stand hearing one more thing that was going to happen to Jack. She was sick to her stomach hearing—He will have a catheter placed in his chest to get chemotherapy. He will lose his hair. He will get radiation burns. The radiation will cause sterility. He will have learning problems. . . . Just as we could barely speak, we had many family and friends wanting us to tell them what was happening with Jack. By unfortunate circumstances we had found out that a good friend of ours was also going through the early diagnosis of brain cancer. They were able to set up a website called Caring Bridge. This is a website designed for people like ourselves who could put information on the web to inform family and friends about the condition of their loved one and provide up-to-date information. As it turned out, writing on this website provided much-needed therapy for us and was an informative tool for our friends and family.

Following are several pages that we wrote on this website as we were going through this time of Jack's illness so that you may better understand how we were feeling at the time:

Journal
Tuesday, May 17, 2005, 9:34 PM CDT

Dear Friends and Family,

We would like to thank-you for your thoughts and prayers and overwhelming emotional and financial support we have received from you.

Today we met with Jack's Pediatric Neuro-Oncologist, Dr. Wetmore. After receiving results of the CT Scans and MRI's Jack was diagnosed with Primitive Neural Ectodermal Tumor (PNET).

From our understanding, A tumor mass could not be located. Apparently, this is very rare. We are still scheduled to meet with several other doctors to devise a treatment plan.

Due to the spreading of the tumor cells on the surface of the brain and spine, Dr. Wetmore recommends high doses of chemo and radiation. Jack will have a stem cell transplant to preserve his immune system. Unfortunately, treatment will not begin for approximately two weeks.

Jack is doing great throughout all of this. He is a pro now and tells the nurses which arm gives the best blood and that if they put the rubber band around his sleeve it doesn't hurt as much. He, also, reassures the MRI nurses that he is not scared and requests the root beer smelling gas mask. We are so proud of his bravery.

All the nurses make sure to comment on his "beautiful long eyelashes."

We will continue to update you and appreciate all of your prayers.

Your support continues to keep us strong.

We learned about this site through a good friend of ours that was diagnosed with a brain tumor in May. Please also keep Jason in your prayers.

God Bless,
Marty and Jen

As you can tell, we felt we were very fortunate to have this tool to be able to communicate with everyone back home with our updates. We were, and still are, so blessed to have so many people pulling for Jack and through this web page we became overwhelmed by the number of people who was pulling for him and joining in on his fight for survival. During the stay in the hospital days would become long and several times a day Jen and I would check his web page to see who had written messages to us in the guest log in section. This would provide for many of laughter and tears for us both.

Journal
Wednesday, May 18, 2005, 11:02 PM CDT

WOW... We can not even begin to express our feelings on the great amount of support we feel when we open up the guest book.

Today was probably the longest day for us since being here. It started with Jack getting a bone scan at 8:00 this morning (which came back normal). The rest of the day was spent meeting with several doctors going over the chemotherapy and radiation schedule for the next few weeks? Although we knew that this was going to be the plan, reality set in when we heard of everything that he would be going through.

Tomorrow Jack will be admitted to St. Mary's hospital at 9:00 to have a Hickman port place in his chest. This port will allow him to receive chemotherapy, draw blood, etc. While he is under sedation they will also collect bone marrow. To our surprise, he will begin chemo on Friday and continue until Sunday. We are hoping and praying he does not become too sick from the chemo. We are looking forward to Ben and Ella visiting us this weekend with Grandma and Grandpa.

God Bless,
Marty and Jen

The doctors at the clinic had a way of making us feel like we were their only concern. If we had questions or just needed to better understand something, they were so patient with us. With Jen's work and education background as a speech therapist and one who works in a hospital she would tend to ask more medical questions and I would tend to ask more of the simple lay-person questions. The entire staff did a great job of providing answers to us that we would both understand.

They understood what we were going through as parents and assured us that Jack was in the best possible hands and it was a "full press" to win this fight. The feeling was that we were handing Jack over to them and trusting them with our son's life. We *were* doing just that and we felt good about it.

Journal
Friday, May 20, 2005 1:06 AM CDT

We really appreciate the support that everyone has given. It is a tremendous help to get through the day when we open up the guest book to see all of the prayers that will help Jack through this.

Today was a pretty long day for Jack. It started out with surgery at 9:00 to place his tube and also to collect marrow. When Jack woke up he was able have a visit from Bailey the hospital golden retriever.

Around 7:00 this evening while Jack was eating he suffered a seizure that required some Valium to bring him out of it. He slept for a little over two hours. When Jack started to wake up he went into another seizure that was more serious. He was transported to the ICU unit where they had to put in a breathing tube to give him a little extra help.

They had taken X-ray's of his chest to find that he had some food that had made it into his lungs during the first seizure. They will be keeping a close eye on this so that he does not get sick from this. If he becomes ill that will delay his chemo treatment.

The staff had also done a CT scan to check to see if Jack had suffered any bleeding of the brain during his seizures. That scan came back normal. So there is a little good news out of all this.

Jack is breathing a lot better now and will hopefully have the tube taken out in the morning.

The staff here at St. Mary's is wonderful. They are so competent in what they were doing and able to keep Jen and me informed every step of the way.

I keep asking myself how much more my little innocent boy needs to endure. But I truly know that God is with Jack and will get him back on the baseball field someday soon.

Thank you again for all your prayers and thoughts.
Keep them coming.
God Bless,
Marty and Jen

This night was one of the longest nights of our lives. When Jack suffered that first seizure he was eating his supper. Dr. Walsh, who is one of the resident doctors, was in our room talking with us when this took place. After Jack fell asleep Jen was worried that he still had food in his throat. Dr. Walsh examined Jack and found nothing.

We then received a visit from Dr. Kottel, who is a Fellow at Mayo. He sat down with Jen and me and told us that if we wanted to move Jack to the ICU unit he would do so, but they were full at the time and Jack would receive good quality care on the regular floor. He would assign Jack his own nurse who would stay at Jack's side. We agreed that he should stay on the regular floor. We were introduced to Nurse Jenny. She was a bubbly, red-headed nurse who was just full of energy and we felt lucky to have her.

After an hour, another nurse came in to get Jack's vitals. This is when I started to notice Jack breathing different. I said something to the nurse and she told me that she would check that out after doing vitals. She then said something that I will never forget, "If he is, that will suck because that will mean more work for me." I looked at Jen and said I thought he was seizing. Jen looked at Jack for one second and said yes he is. She then looked at the nurse and told her to get some help. By this time Jack was starting to convulse and turning blue. We were looking at the nurse while she was fumbling about. She then looked at us and said, "He needs oxygen, give him some oxygen!" Jen and I looked at each other like "What the hell is going on?" The nurse then hit the code blue button. Alarms were going off and within 20 seconds we had fifteen people in our room working on Jack. At Jack's head was Dr. Walsh. I remember looking around the room and not knowing anyone. I held Jen in my arms as they worked on Jack. They were sucking saliva out of Jack's mouth while giving him a sedative to calm his convulsions. As they worked sucking the saliva out something clogged the tube. One of the doctors asked, "What was that?" "A green bean!" said Dr. Walsh. I remember her glance, she looked at Jen with acknowledgement that Jen was right about the food in his throat and at the same time the glance was an apology for missing it. Dr. Walsh then proceeded to put the breathing tube into Jack's throat. As they were doing this I kept on looking out into the hallway because there were all these people standing around. I noticed a man in a suit who had complete focus on Jen and me. I wondered who this man was, was he an administrator? And if so, I have some words for him later!

As soon as they were able to get Jack calmed down we transported him to the ICU unit. This would be our first of many trips there and we were unsure of what to expect. They wheeled him into his room where we met Nurse Tom. We listened to all of the updates that one doctor would pass along to the other with great interest so that not one thing would be left out in our memories.

Because St. Mary's is a teaching hospital, the head doctors would look to the residents to ask their opinions and then give them a nod in agreement or a suggestion if they differed, all of this done with respect toward each other. Tom would also give his opinions. This was quit different for us to see because we had never witnessed an occasion when a nurse had this much to say about a patient. We knew we were in good hands now.

Nurse Jen showed up at the door with our belongings from our old room. She had tears in her eyes and said she was so sorry that she was not there. Another patient needed their wraps changed and that she was the only one that could do it. You could tell in her eyes that she hurt inside. We assured her it was not her fault and that we understood.

By this time the man in the suit that I had seen out in the hallway approached Jen and me. He introduced himself as Warren, one of the hospital chaplains. We greeted him and spoke with him for a long time about where we were from and about Jack's illness. To this day I don't know what religion Warren is affiliated with and it doesn't matter. He was there in a time of need for us and let us pray with him the way we wanted to pray.

When all was settled and the lights went to a dim Nurse Tom looked at Jen and me and said, "I have a sleep room for one of you and the other can sleep in here." Going to sleep was not an option and I would be by Jack's side all night long. I told Jen to go to the sleep room and try to get some rest and that I would come get her if anything happened.

With just Tom and me in the room I told him I needed to get something off my chest or I was not going to be able to sleep. He turned to me and assured me that I could tell him anything. I told him what the nurse had said about Jack creating more work for her and how she had acted. I told him that I wasn't trying to get anyone fired, but if there was a loose link in the chain, she was it and it almost cost my son his life. Tom assured me that he would make sure that it would not go unnoticed. We never saw that nurse again on the pediatric unit.

After my conversation with Tom I decided to go and check on Jen to see if she was ok. What actually happened when I got into the room was that I broke down like a little baby. I fell into Jen's arms and wept. I thought about all of the times when Jack would ask to play ball and I would say, "How about tomorrow?" I thought about how many times I would stay one extra hour at work or stay out with the guys for one more beer and get home after he was asleep. Would I ever get to play ball with him again? Jen was my comforter that evening.

We both finally fell asleep and woke up the next morning around 7:00 a.m. We ran to Jack's room feeling guilty that one of us was not there. When we reached the room there was another nurse sitting in his room on the computer. She informed us that they already did their shift change and Tom said that Jack slept all night long with ease.

Before rounds started Dr. Walsh came into our room and sat on the edge of the bed. She asked us how we felt about the previous night. She told us that she was sorry for missing the green bean. We assured her that we did not feel any ill feelings towards her or the staff. We told her we were just amazed that she was able to stay so focused and put Jack's breathing tube in his throat while we were looking on after she had sucked that bean from his throat. When Dr. Walsh left the room Jen and I talked about what a good doctor she was going to be.

Journal

Saturday, May 21, 2005, 8:03 AM CDT

Jack was able to get the breathing tube out around 8:30 Friday morning and has been breathing on his own with ease. He was pretty tired from the night before and was able to sleep all day Friday.

In between the teams of doctors checking on Jack it was a pretty quiet day. Jack woke up around 7:00 last night wanting Ice Cream and Pizza. We knew we had our Jack back.

We are hoping to move back to his regular room today.

Ben and Ella made a visit with Grandma and Grandpa Hoeger yesterday and were able to see Jack for a little while. I took Ben back to the Ronald McDonald house with me for the night.

Today Jack will begin his chemo treatments.

The phrase Onward and Upward had not meant so much before.

God Bless,
Marty and Jen

One of another struggles of our life during this time was not being able to see Ben and Ella every day. We talked to them every day but it was the little things that we missed. When you think about what is involved in 1- and 3- year-old's lives, that can be pretty significant. It was a fact of life that we both needed to be there for Jack and having Ben and Ella there was not an option at this point.

Journal
Tuesday, May 24, 2005, 8:06 PM CDT

We are happy to say that Wellmark called yesterday and approved the stem cell transplant. We are uncertain if it was the letter that Jack's doctor sent or the threat of Bryan and Sean storming the lawn naked. Either way we are very relieved.

One thing that we have realized is that there is no planning ahead for anything. We met with the doctors last night and were ready to be discharged today. But, Jack had a hard night last night feeling sick to his stomach and got very little sleep. When we woke up at 7:30, Jack was in the middle of a seizure. Later he suffered another one and needed sedation to stop the seizure activity. He has been resting all day and is currently on EEG monitors for the rest of the night.

We are hoping that they are able to get the seizure medicine under control, SOON. Now, we are at the point where we are taking it one day at a time.

Many people have asked where to send cards. We feel that it would be best to send them to our home and we can get them from family members who visit.

The one constant thing that gets us through the day is when we pull up Jack's web page and see all the thoughts and prayers from so many people.

God Bless and give your loved ones extra hugs.

Marty and Jen

Back when we had our first visit with Dr. Wetmore she had informed us that in Jack's treatment plan he would go through what they call a Stem Cell Transplant. It was a procedure that would have to take place for Jack to survive. She told us that some insurance companies think of this as an "experimental" procedure and therefore will not cover the cost. When she walked in the room that day and gave us the news that insurance would cover the procedure, we were overwhelmed with hopeful feelings and we really thought that things were going in the right direction now and we couldn't wait to proceed with his treatment plan. We wanted to get started right away—but the cancer that had taken over Jack's body had other plans.

Chapter 6
One Left-Handed Hug

Journal
Wednesday, May 25, 2005, 8:44 PM CDT

Your continued support has helped us through yet another difficult day with Jack and his illness. He was hooked up to the EEG monitor last night to monitor his seizure activity. It was noticed at 3:00 a.m. that he was not moving his right side. At that time, Jack had a CT scan to rule out a brain bleed. The CT was normal.

Throughout the day, Jack was unable to communicate to us verbally or move his right side. We met with the oncologist tonight and she is optimistic that it is a temporary result of the brain tumor. The next 48 hours will be critical for us to control his seizures so that his body has the ability to bounce back.

Today was filled with many emotional ups and downs. By reading this website it helps us to regroup for another day.

God Bless,

Marty and Jen

This was by far the hardest day for me. I would look into Jack's eyes and he knew something was wrong. He wanted so badly to say something but he couldn't. He wanted to move but couldn't. His eyes were filled with pain and fear. I felt so helpless. I was his dad, someone who was to always protect him and all I could do was stand there and tell him that it was going to be OK. Not knowing if it was really going to be OK or not, I'm sure he could probably see through that. We had to resort to putting a pull-up diaper on Jack because we were not able transport him to the bathroom in a timely matter with all of the equipment that he was hooked up to and he was unable to communicate with us. When we put the diaper on he closed his eyes and began to cry. His cry was so painful, tears ran down his face and the tone in his voice was that of a moan. He turned his head and would not look at Jen or me. It was like he had gone into a deep depression. This just tore me apart inside. I was standing there totally helpless while Jack was engaging in the fight for his life.

When Dr. Wetmore came into our room that day and I confronted her with our feeling that some of the other doctors who visited Jack left us with a very negative outlook. Dr. Wetmore was always very upbeat and confident. She told us that this would be temporary and that Jack would bounce back. I looked at her and told her that I wanted to know the facts and prepare myself for the worst. What should we prepare for? She looked at me with a straight face and said, "I am not here to be your cheerleader. I am here to save Jack's life and make sure he leads as normal a life as he can." From that time on we took Dr. Wetmore at her word and would never question her positive outlook on Jack's future.

Journal
Thursday, May 26, 2005, 10:24 PM CDT

Today was a day of lessons for us:

Lesson # 1

Jack received a visit from his neurologist this morning. I vented some frustration about Jack's progress. He taught me that this is a battle of inches not feet. So, when Jack wiggled his right toe today, that was the inch we were looking for.

Lesson #2

One left-handed hug can mean as much as one million two handed hugs. Amazingly, he seems to hug us to console us.

Lesson #3

How much 6 straight hours of sleep, a warm shower and a walk on a nice day can clear a person's mind.

Lesson #4

We know now why Minnesota has 10,000 lakes. It has rained every day since we have been here.

We will be seeing Ben and Ella again this weekend for our much needed therapy. Thank you all for helping us get through another day.

God Bless,
Marty and Jen

Jack's neurologist is a very pleasant man. He walks the halls of Mayo and St. Mary's in a small frame but with a large heart. He sat us down and encouraged us not to be dismayed and reminded us that even though Jack was a fighter he was not in a fight, but rather a marathon. He would have steps that were harder than others but when all was said and done we would have to be positive that he would see the finish line.

I often wonder how we were lucky enough to get the doctors that we had. They seemed to know what we needed to hear at just the right times. We made a commitment that day that if Jack was not going to give up then we were not going to give up on him either. That day I looked into Jack's eyes and told him how proud of him I was and that I would help him fight to get better again. At that moment Jack lifted his left arm and put it around my neck and pulled me to him and squeezed me tight against him. He gave me the best ONE HANDED HUG a person could ever ask for. That feeling is with me still to this day.

Journal
Saturday, May 28, 2005, 9:17 PM CDT

A couple of days ago, we shared with you about the many lessons we learned going through this rough time. Last night, we learned a very important lesson…God does things on his own and when he wants to do them, even if it is at 4:00 a.m.

About 9:00 last night, we were meeting with one of the doctors about Jack and shared with her our concerns about his eyesight and twitching in his right side. We were trying to decide if it was seizure activity or voluntary movement. Nobody was quite sure. Six hours later, I was woken up by one of the nurses saying that Jack wanted me. He was wide awake, so I climbed in bed with him for a while. Then, out of the blue, he looks at me and says "I want Mom"! Imagine how high I jumped out of bed to retrieve Jen. It will be a moment in my life that I will never forget!

Jack still has trouble talking, but he is able to get out some words and sometimes a couple of words together. He was able to say Hi to Grandma Sis and Aunt Amy on the phone today. To add to his achievements today, he is moving his right leg and arm purposefully.

Today was not a progress by inches – it was progress by YARDS!

Ben and Ella made the trip today and provided their own bit of therapy for all three of us. As soon as Ben stepped into the room Jack's eyes lit up and he just about jumped out of bed towards him. It didn't take long for Ben to spot the Scooby-Doo ball and want to play catch with Jack. Jack was able to throw with his left hand and even tried a couple of times with his right. Yet another moment I will never forget. I feel that we owe such a big part of this to all of you that are thinking and praying for Jack everyday. We could never get through this without our friends and family.

We would like to wish good luck to Dr. Erin and Dr. Andy, and send out a special thanks to them and the team of doctors that will be leaving for their next rotation. We are sad to see them go. They have seen Jen and me at our lowest of low and were always there to listen and answer all of our questions.

Please say an extra prayer for our friend Jason who starts radiation on Tuesday, as well as for our little buddy Conner.

God Bless,

Marty and Jen

We were filled with so many doubts about what our future held with Jack. Would he ever walk again? Would he ever speak again? Why would God have him suffer so much if he was to die from cancer? Jen and I went through so many feelings about not wanting to give up the fight but we also did not want to see him suffer any longer. We would feel so guilty for feeling like this. How could the thought of him dying ever enter our minds? Are we giving up on him? We would go through these emotions and talk to each other and vowed that whatever our feelings were we needed to be honest with each other and we would help each other get through this. We both believe in the value of life and how it should be lived to the fullest. Was this going to be his quality of life? No matter what happened, time and time again, Jack would show us that he was not going to give up and neither should we.

Journal
Wednesday, June 1, 2005, 7:53 AM CDT

Good morning,

It is strange to update the journal in the morning; unfortunately we had no choice because the website was down last night.

I think that Jack has been seizure free for 24 hours! Yippee! His day was much calmer yesterday. We continue to fight with keeping that seizure medicine level at an appropriate level. Also, he had a blood and platelet transfusion yesterday.

Since Jack seemed better, I took a break to do some browsing at "TJ Max and More" (my new favorite store). It felt wonderful to be more than 3 blocks from the hospital. I was on a mission to buy Jack a cool hat, since in a couple of days he'll really need it. I was lucky to find a Nike hat that looks like one of Marty's, so he especially liked it.

We are going on a trip to Mayo clinic today. Jack will be fitted for his radiation mask this morning. We are not sure if they will have to sedate him or not for the procedure. We hope not, because sedation usually causes a lot of problems for Jack. But, Jack is excited because the trip will involve an ambulance ride-- this one he'll actually remember.

Yesterday, Jack stood on the scale by himself! He is so weak and fragile, but getting BETTER! His little voice is so soft it is difficult to hear him. He still has a lot of frustration with the lack of communication, but we are getting it figured out. The doctors feel that even after the first day of radiation, we could see some pretty good results. Unfortunately, when the radiation kills off the tumor cells, the brain will have more inflammation and will cause more seizures. This should get better through once these dirty, rotten (*^*&%*#%&%^&^ tumor cells are destroyed. We haven't been told yet when the radiation will actually begin--sooner than they thought originally though.

Jack slept pretty good last night, which means so did Marty and I! Thank Goodness because the night before, Jack was so upset that he only calmed when Marty and I BOTH slept with him. Imagine that tight squeeze!

Thanks for tuning in again for an update in the Hoeger Hospital reality show!

Please check out the new photos!

God Bless you all,

Jen and Marty

We were anxious to get the radiation procedure started. We felt that this was the next step in Jack's marathon. Because St. Mary's Hospital is located about 1 mile from Mayo Clinic where they did the radiation procedure, we would transport Jack via ambulance every day. We were able to get to know the EMT staff fairly well. One night Jack became bothered by his hair falling out onto his pillow and scratching him. So Jen got out the clippers to give him a trim. Jack asked if he could do it himself. With a little trepidation Jen let him. Jack had a ball. With a nurse on one side and Jen on the other Jack shaved away. Although this was a "new look" and took a little time to get used to, Jack was happy and proud of his new and improved hairdo that he had given to himself.

I can only imagine what it is like for someone who has cancer to go through the process of loosing their hair. My only advice to them is to not let it fall out, shave it off and remove the hair on your own terms. To this date, because of the side effects of radiation three years later,

Jack's hair has come back in some spots but mostly he is still bald. He is fine with it and has never complained and he brags about how he cuts his own hair!

Journal
Tuesday, June 7, 2005, 10:00 PM CDT

As much as we appreciate all the prayers, I hope you will also remember to thank God for answering our prayers. We don't want to keep asking for "stuff" and not remembering to express our gratitude.

Well, the morning started off with Jack's feeding tube coming out of his nose following him getting sick. So we made the decision to just pull it out and TRY to get him to take all the medicine orally (12 medicines in total) AND keep it down. That little boy sure keeps amazing us, because as hard as it was he tried several times and eventually kept it down!

Jack is working hard with physical therapy, showing off how he can shoot baskets. He is showing the occupational therapist how he can color using his right hand. Each day he gets stronger! We just began the fight and yet we feel we have conquered so much.

Jack asked me "Do you have a day off tomorrow?" (a common question when we are at home) I laughed and said "Yes mommy will have lots of days off." Please realize that thanks to all of you, we can afford to be with our son during the most critical time in his life and we will be grateful forever!

In honor of the feeding tube removal, we wanted to celebrate with his favorite Chinese meal (sorry Jason we couldn't wait for you). Unfortunately, when Marty was retrieving our supper, Jack suffered a seizure. Unfortunately, Jack needed to be sedated to end the seizure. SO-- we put the chicken fried rice in the refrigerator and will heat it up when he wakes up—no matter what time that may be.

Radiation begins tomorrow at 10:00 a.m. They say that with radiation, Jack will have more seizures. It will be interesting to see what the next 24 hours will be like. Although we are nervous for more seizures, we know that the only way to get through this is to get the radiation started.

Even though our night was not what we expected, we can't stop thinking about how good our day was! Keep the faith, say a prayer, and don't forget to thank God.

Jen and Marty

The neurology department worked so hard to get Jack's seizure levels under control. This is the true meaning of practicing medicine. They would take his blood levels every day to see where they were. Sometimes he would be too high on one drug and to low on the other so they would play with the doses to try to get all the levels at a therapeutic rate.

Our mornings would start out with the oncology department coming in together on rounds and discussing Jack's last 24 hours, and then we would receive a visit from the neurology department to go over his blood levels and they would let us know what they were going to change. At one point Jack was on 12 different seizure medicines. They would add a new drug and take away another one and each time it had to happen gradually. Every time we met with a new doctor or a new resident they would ask for the up-to-date changes in medicine. It would get really confusing sometimes and most of the time it was extremely frustrating.

We were receiving so much support from home. People were sending cards, emails, and phone calls. Jack thought it was Christmas almost every time Grandma and Grandpa showed up because they had toys, books, and stuffed animals from people who wanted to do something but felt helpless. Jen and I would receive cards with money, gift cards to McDonalds, gas cards—everything you can imagine—people gave. When Jen and I would trade off going home people would bring over meals so that we could just spend our time with Ben and Ella. There would be times that we would check out of a hotel and the desk manager would say that the bill was paid for. A special friend from home would call up and pay for our hotel on several occasions. One time we switched hotels because we felt guilty and somehow they found out where we were staying and did it again.

Friends from our church planned a special prayer service for Jack one night and almost packed the church to pray as a community to join in his fight. It was just so overwhelming how much support we were receiving and we didn't even know that it was just the tip of the iceberg.

Journal
Thursday June 9, 2005, 9:16 PM CDT

For all of the bad days that you have read on this site, we are so excited to share with you the good days.

Today marked our 3 week anniversary in the hospital. Not one to be proud of, but when we look back to all that has happened we are sure proud of everything Jack has overcome in 3 short weeks.

Today was his best day since we got here. It began with Jack eating a full bagel, as well as half of mom's. During physical therapy, Jack was able to play baseball in the atrium with very little assistance. It won't be long and he will be hitting the ball field soon.

For lunch, we took Jack to the park for a picnic! He played on the swings and play set for a short time. While at the park, Jen and I had played back in our minds how we were so excited two weeks ago when he was able to wiggle his fingers and toes.

When we returned from the park, we found a gift on Jack's bed from Darryl and Tom (the ambulance drivers that transported Jack back and forth form the hospital to the Mayo Clinic). They had given Jack a Twins hat. Even though it's not the Cubs, we figured we can root for both teams. Now-- if they both play in the World Series, then some serious decisions will have to be made!

We are constantly reminded how special Jack is. He has been able to wrap the nurses and staff around his little finger with his smile and determination to beat this disease.

We would like to thank all of you who continue to make this journey with us. We hope that you, also, have been able to share in the good days – ESPECIALLY since it has been all of you who got us through the past 3 weeks!

God Bless,
Marty and Jen

This was just one more example of Jack's determination to get better. He had been knocked down so many times but he kept getting up to fight harder and push through that wall that marathon runners talk about. What a thrill to see him stand in that atrium and hit that Nerf ball again and again (a couple went over the railing onto the second floor!). In the atrium on the third floor there is a large two-story painted glass window that was letting the sun beam through. I felt like a dad watching his son playing in the World Series.

After three weeks of what seemed like nothing but bad news being reported we were able to finally put some good news on the web page. That day while we were typing it felt like we opened the window at St. Mary's and shouted it all the way to Cedar Rapids.

Since we had been in Rochester for some time now, we were able to find a nice park that was a fairly close drive to the hospital. It had a large playset that had one bridge attached to another. Jack would sit in the swing and just laugh, go down the slides, and he moved around very easily. When we returned to the hospital and discovered the hat that Darryl and Tom had left it just "capped off" the perfect day! Was the worst now behind us?

Jack at age 5 before Cancer

One of the first days at Mayo

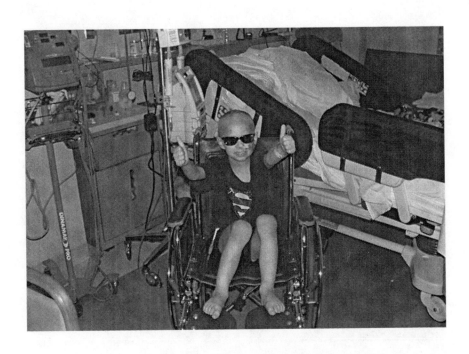

Chemo starting to effect his body but not his spirit.

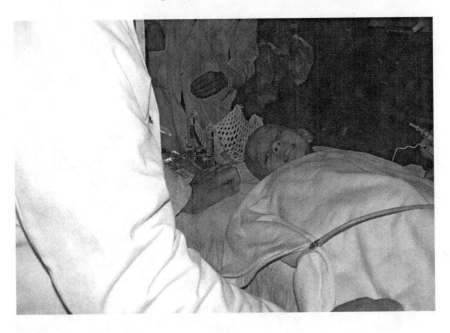

Jack getting ready for radiation

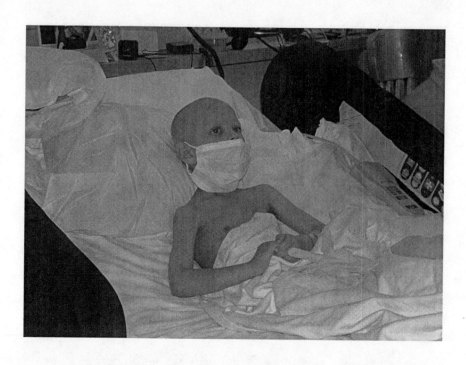

Jack in the sterilzation wing getting ready for Stem Cell harvest

Jack in physical therapy hitting the ball over the railing

Jack playing baseball for YMCA the summer of 2008

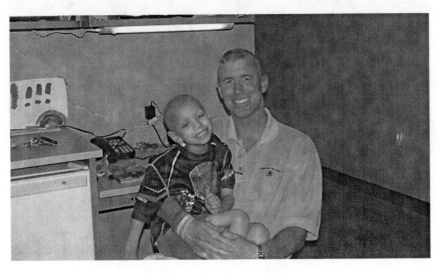

Jack with his guardian angel Jason Hill

Team JackStrong has raised over $8,000 in two years for Relay for Life!

Chapter 8
Our New Home—the Ronald McDonald House

Journal
Wednesday, June 15, 2005, 6:41 PM CDT

We are officially residents of the Ronald McDonald house! It is like being in college all over again, minus the cocktails!

All the families are super nice and we are quickly making friends. Even Jack has found other 5 year olds to hang out with. It is a different world in this house—kids with feeding tubes and kids without hair is normal. The common question is "So what does he have?" I have always tried to live life with the philosophy that "Life could be worse". Just when I thought our "life could not be any worse" I meet those in more difficult situations. For example, I met a family that is from the Middle East and have not been home for 3 months (they have a 6 year old back home) and another family from Turkey. I know how lucky we are to be only 3 short hours from Ben, Ella and home.

Jack and I were very busy this morning. I woke him up at 4:00 am to take medicine (which did not go well) so I had to wake him up at 5:00 to try again (successfully). We were at Mayo from 6:45 am until 11:30 am. Then believe it or not, I actually cooked lunch (the first time in 6 weeks)! Definitely a feast of Mac-n-cheese! The rest of the day was spent shopping for a Fathers Day gift and of course something little for the kids. You can tell Jack is getting a lot better when he can keep up with me shopping.

While awake this morning at 4:00, I thought about how dark those days were when Jack had every bit of quality of life taken from him. I realized that we were what seemed like, a step away from the worst. It felt like being in the deepest part of a valley and then I realized that maybe we needed to get to the lowest point to get a running start UP the mountain! It feels so good to be climbing towards the top. Hopefully by Memorial Day weekend 2006 we will be at the top defeating cancer. "God only gives you, what you can handle?" Right?!

God Bless you,
Jen

This was a very special place and time in our lives during Jack's battle with cancer. We were now residents of the wonderful community of the Ronald McDonald House. It was an eye-opening experience for us. While at St. Mary's Hospital we were in our own little world and our only concern was Jack and getting him better. At times we felt like we were being punished for something. Then we moved into "the house" and saw that we were not the only ones going through this. Yes, every situation is different and everyone there had their own issues to deal with, but what we thought was bad was really not so bad.

I could not imagine going through this experience without having the Ronald McDonald House as part of it. It got us through a lot of tough times in Rochester and hopefully some day we will be able to give back tenfold.

This was also a defining moment in our marriage. We would trade off days of being home. I would stay with Jack Monday thru Wednesday and Jen would come up on Wednesday thru Friday. Then she would drive home with Jack and then I would take Jack back on Sunday nights. In Marriage Encounter this is what they call being "Married Single." It was what we needed to do at the time and what we felt was best for the kids and we felt blessed that we were only three hours away and able to have that arrangement.

Journal
Thursday, June 16, 2005, 8:16 PM CDT

Hello,

Jack continues to have good nights and days! I experimented with how I presented his medicine last night (actually early morning) and it worked. I had to wake him up 3 times, but we managed. The radiation guys and gals are so impressed with how Jack walks into the radiation room, jumps on the bed and kindly asks for a warm blanket (it is very frigid in those rooms, right Jason?). They are getting his sedation dosage to a better level so that he wakes up within ½ hour of his treatment. AND still NO seizures!

You know how you hear how people can see "god through other people," well I have been witnessing that since day one up here-but especially last night! Jack has been befriended by a 12 year-old named Austin. Austin is here with his brother Sean (who is a 16 year old fighting cancer). Anyway, Jack has been pretty shy, especially since he sometimes has a hard time finding his words (unlike his mother who always finds plenty :), but this sweet Austin has taken Jack under his wing. He says "hey buddy do you want to play video games", he'll give him a penny, and even had Jack RUNNING down the halls (I was a little freaked, but enjoyed the uncoordinated site). But when Austin heard that Jack had trouble keeping his medicine down, he said "come here buddy I will help you". So Austin cheered Jack on pill by pill and he kept them down. I believe that is what is meant by seeing "god through others".

Jack and I received a wonderful visit from our friend Courtney who was traveling through town with her husband. We laughed a lot and had a good lunch. She helped me out by sitting with Jack in the van while I ran into Wal-Mart to do my pharmacy "stuff" (we all know how fast Wal-Mart can be-no offense). While I was in the store, Courtney gave Jack a game and taught him how to play. Jack had a blast and actually it is a great learning tool also! Thanks again Courtney for a fun afternoon. We are super excited for Marty and Batman Ben to come tomorrow. AS WELL AS, Grandma Sis, Papa Tom, Uncle Bob and Aunt Julie.

I hope you all are having a great day and know that I thank God for you all every night.

PS – Please say a prayer for Austin's brother, Sean, who gets checked on Friday to see if the cancer is gone—if so he gets to "blow this popstand!".

God Bless,
Jen

When Jack was going through radiation while we lived at the RMH we would have to get up early in the morning to give him his meds early enough. Because he was being sedated every day, he could not have anything in his stomach. A bus would pick us up every day at 7:15 so that we could make his 8:00 radiation appointment. Once we were there we would check in at the counter then go sit in the room and wait with the other 20 to 30 people in the waiting room.

One day after they had taken Jack back to his room, I was in the waiting room and an elderly lady walked up to me and asked me about Jack and his illness. As I told her his story her eyes welled up with tears.

She then told me that she was sorry but had to share with me that since her husband was diagnosed he had been a very bitter man. He would not go to church anymore and felt like God had cheated him in life. She then proceeded to tell me that on their way home yesterday they were talking about Jack and wondered what he had. Her husband then broke down and cried to her, telling her he felt so guilty that he was acting like this when there was a 5-year-old boy who was being cheated out of so much life that *he* had already been able to live. She then said that at that time he vowed to be positive and upbeat no matter what lay ahead. He said to his wife, "If that little boy can smile every day he comes in then why can't I."

That day I looked at Jack and his illness in a whole new light. Before, I was so focused on what we were doing that I never realized the effect that he was having on the people around him. Now, when I walked through the halls of the Mayo Clinic I would notice people's faces as they looked at Jack with his little bald head and it was if they seemed to understand that life could be worse.

I also wondered why Jack was so good during all of this. He would have his moments of being sad but most of the time he took everything in stride. I wondered if he didn't understand what was going on. I wondered if that was just his personality coming out, that he was a fighter and nothing was going to keep him down. Whatever it was I am sure that many people saw God thru Jack.

Jack's radiation team was fabulous. They really took time to get to know him and our family. They made this a very enjoyable time for Jack, what he would call his "sleep test." He looked forward to it every day. They would give him the warmest blankets and make him feel like a rock star.

Again, we felt lucky that we received the best that Mayo had to offer.

Journal
Monday, June 20, 2005 8:22, PM CDT

Hello,

This morning Jack had his catheter placed in his neck and started the stem cell harvest. Earlier in the morning, we had to find a way to creatively explain to him what was going to occur. So, we explained that since he had so much energy, he would have a special tube put in his neck so that a special medicine could take his extra "power cells" out. Then, the doctors would freeze his "power cells" and they would put them back in his body through his special tube if he ever got really sick. Then, the "power cells" would reenergize him again. Amazingly, he thought it sounded pretty cool!

When he woke up from the sedation and felt the discomfort in his neck, he had big crocodile tears and "Dad, I want to get out of here!" Marty promised him that if he stayed strong, we would go home this weekend for a party... A BIG party!

Speaking of promises, back in the "dark days" of our hospital stay when Jack was miserable – out of EXTREME DESPERATION – we promised Jack a dog. Yes, a DOG! (I'm sure Grandma Rosie is laughing and Grandma Sis is gasping.) Jack has wanted a dog pretty much since he could say "dog." Fortunately, for a few years, I was able to put it off by saying "Oh, honey we are going to have a baby, instead!" So if anyone has any dog advice for us, we would appreciate it. Of course, I would prefer a small, quiet, calm, nonshedding, potty-trained dog!

All in all, Jack did very well during the 5 hour harvest. The process made him tired, so Jack and I caught up on some sleep and Marty caught up with some party poker. The plan is to harvest again in the morning, so please say a prayer that we get enough stem cells by tomorrow evening.

Make sure to see the updated photos!

Enjoy your day and God Bless,
Jen and Marty

Leading up to the stem cell transplant we were to give Jack a shot in the leg every day for five days. This shot would help him produce cells at a rapid rate to ensure that they would collect enough cells to store. We would take Jack to the infusion center to administer the shot and to get a transfusion of platelets and blood. On the fourth day of the shot the nurse looked at the bottle and noticed that something was wrong. She called down to the pharmacist and they discovered that whoever was giving the dosage was reading the conversion chart wrong and that Jack was only receiving half of the dosage that was ordered. The last two days he received what he was supposed to. Our goal was to collect 15 million cells so that he would receive 5 million after each round of high-dose chemo—three in total. After the first day we were informed that they had only collected 1 million cells.

For this procedure they placed a tube in the left side of his neck that would draw his blood out of his body. Then it would go through a large machine that would separate the stem cells from his blood and then put the blood back into another tube in his neck. You could see the stem cells being collected in a clear bag next to the machine.

The second day they informed us that they were only able to collect another 3 million, not nearly enough to even do one dose of chemo. They told us that they would release Jack from the hospital and we were to continue on with the radiation treatment and we would try again after radiation was complete. We felt defeated. I felt like what seemed like a mistake from the pharmacist cheated Jack out of what may have been the only thing that would save his life.

Journal
Sunday, June 27, 2005 10:58 AM CDT

THANK – YOU FROM THE BOTTOM OF OUR HEARTS FOR ALL THOSE THAT HAVE ORGANIZED, DONATED, AND ATTENDED THE AMAZING BENEFIT FOR JACKSON!

We really do not know what to say other than THANK YOU! The benefit on Saturday for Jack was anything but "a little get together".

When we parked and started to walk up the lane and we were greeted by the Horsefields who drove up from Davenport and the Novak's who drove up from Kansas City we knew we were in for a special evening.

The prayer service began with some nice music and ended with some touching words from Jen. It is far easier for me to hide behind this computer than to get up and say these things in public, so for that I thank her for having the courage to do it for the both of us. She had me in tears and I knew what she was going to say.

There are so many things about that evening that we will never forget and will be forever grateful for. Here a couple that stick out that still brings smiles:

Jack playing soccer in the yard with all his friends

Batman driving down the lane to pick up Jack and Ben for a ride in the Bat mobile.

The CRFD driving all the way out to give Jack a ride with his special friend Sam Lorimer in the fire truck.

Joe Fandel finding his calling in life as an auctioneer.
(Thank you Joe)

Hailey Dolphin receiving her first car at age 5

We would like to thank everyone who had spent countless hours of preparing for the event and the Hiserotes for offering up their beautiful home. (You must have had a good Realtor).

JACKS BIRTHDAY

Today is Jacks 6th birthday

It was kicked off at 6:45 with my employer True North Companies offering to fly us back to Rochester in their company plane. Jack, Ben and I made the trip up north in 40 minutes. (New record time)

Jack then introduced Brother Ben to all the nurses and doctors who give Jack radiation everyday. Jack was anxious to show Ben his own mask and where he goes everyday for a nap.

After lunch we made a trip north to Camp Snoopy with Cousin Dana where we spent a couple hours riding rides and eating supper at the Rain Forest Café.

Now it's back to the grind for another week fighting Cancer and making more memories.

God Bless,
Marty and Jen

While Jen and I were in Rochester with Jack there were some rumors floating around that some of our friends and family members were going to plan a benefit on Jack's behalf. When I first heard about this I was absolutely against it and did not want any part of it. I even made a couple of phone calls to encourage people not to be spending so much time and energy on this. I then received some advice from a good friend. The advice was that so many people read Jack's website and feel helpless and that this was a way for them to help out. Me not wanting it was being selfish on my own part because this is what they wanted so I should let them do it for Jack.

Well, the benefit just blew us away. They started it off with a nice prayer service. They had four bands lined up to play, and a kid's carnival set up, a silent auction, and a live auction. So many people from our community stepped up to help with so many donations it was overwhelming. Most of all it was a day for us to see so many of our friends and family members again that we were not able to see for almost a year.

This benefit was a gift sent from above. We would have never made it through the year financially without it and it gave us the breathing room we needed to get by. I knew we would never be able to thank people enough for their generosity, but hopefully them seeing Jack surviving this would help them feel like they were a major part of it because they were and still are today.

Chapter 9
Beating Spencer

Journal
Tuesday, June 28, 2005 PM CDT

One of the things that has amazed both Jen and me is the fact that Jack has never asked the question WHY.

Not why this is happening to him? Not why are we always in the hospital? Not even why is he so sick all of the time? Until last night, I guess he felt that he was six now and he is old enough to know.

Last night before bed Jack asked why he has to go to the doctors every day for tests. I reminded him of all the headaches that he used to have and that the doctors are making sure that the headaches go away forever. He then asked who gave him the headaches. I explained to him that he is a very special boy and that God had given him something called Cancer and we needed to go to the doctors and get rid of it. He then asked why God gave cancer to him. I told him that God had picked him because he knew that Jack was a super tough boy and that he was strong enough to beat cancer.

Jack informed me that he was tough enough to beat cancer because he liked to exercise and do Tae Bo with mom. He asked if I'd call mom and tell her to make sure to bring all of the tapes with her so they could exercise.

He then asked if mom would be there to help him beat cancer. I let him know that everyone at the party was there to help him and everyone that reads about him on the computer are going to be there to help him beat cancer.

He then asked if Brad with the big muscles was going to help him. I said yes…That brought a big smile on his face. He informed me that maybe uncle Denny would help him because he was a strong fireman. I assured him that uncle Denny was for sure going to help him.

The first thing he said this morning was if "Spencer" was still in his head. I said "No Jack you mean cancer" he said well I forgot that word so can I call him Spencer? Sorry for any of you named Spencer but Jack is on a mission to beat you.

Today while meeting with one of the doctors Ben hit his head and Jack told him to be careful so that Spencer does not get into his head. The doctor gave a smile and Jack informed her that Spencer was in hiding in his head and that he needed to take his medicine and exercise so that he would go away.

I never realized how smart six year olds were.

God Bless to all of you and thank you for joining us in Jacks fight against SPENCER!

Marty and Jen

As I think back to that conversation I remember being on the bottom bunk in our room of the RMH. He asked me those questions and I kept thinking to myself, "How could I tell him that he was battling a disease that millions of people die from every year. How can I tell him so that he understands, when I don't even understand it myself?" To this point Jack had never asked WHY and I was asking this question 20 times a day for almost a year now!

When Jack could finally put a name on what was wrong with him all bets were off, he was on a mission. He could not wait to start his Tae Bo and he would yell out "BYE-BYE Spencer." It was better than any of the Rocky scenes Hollywood could come up with. Just imagine a 30-pound bald kid doing Tae Bo in a muscle man shirt and it would be enough to make anyone want to join the fight!

Martin A. Hoeger

Journal
Tuesday, July 12, 2005, 10:01 PM CDT

*ARMSTONG BLOWS AWAY COMPETITION ON TOUGH
MOUNTAINOUS RIDE!*

*I can't help but think that there is a reason why we have people like
Lance Armstrong in this world to teach us that giving up is not an option.*

*Today, I met with the radiation doctors to learn the results of Jack's MRI.
The cancer cells in the spinal area seem to be reacting well to radiation. The
cells in the brain however have not been reduced as much as the doctors
would like to see. Therefore, we will be doing an additional two weeks of
radiation after this Friday.*

*After we met with the radiation doctors it was off to the Oncology dept
to go over the lab work that was done on Jack this morning. We learned
that his cell counts were low and we were off to St. Mary's Hospital for a
platelet transfusion. We also are giving Jack a shot called GCSF which is a
steroid booster to help produce some good cells. Tomorrow after radiation
we will return to St. Mary's where Jack will receive a blood transfusion at
12:00.*

*We finally returned back to our room around 5:30 and after a short
rest time and supper Jack handed me the Tae Bo tape and said he needed*

94

to exercise. I guess Jack is also here to show us that giving up is not an option.

God Bless and Livestrong!

Marty and Jen

We soon found out that the original plan of having six weeks of radiation was not going to cut it, so they added on another two weeks, which would concentrate entirely on the brain. This was taking a toll on Jack's body. His skin was breaking down as if he had a sunburn. We would change the dressings on his stomach a couple of times a day and rub ointment on his burns. His head was turning a yellowish-brown color. When we would return to the RMH he would be dressed in a sweatsuit and always ask for a warm blanket. We eventually would get him a heating pad to lie on to keep him warm. All of this in JULY! To this day Jack is not a fan of the winter and still has some side effects from the radiation.

Chapter 10
Our Summer—At Last!

Journal
Tuesday, July 26, 2005, 10:12 PM CDT

NO MORE RADIATION – EVER!

I couldn't fight back the tears when we walked down the long radiation hallway to see our "dream team" for the last time. They congregated around Jack and presented him with many presents. I made sure to tell them that they needed to always remember that they have made a difference in Jack's life! Goodbye to Desk R and our dream team, we will never forget you.

Jack's blood work resulted in him needing platelets and a blood transfusion. He was also nutropenic, which means his cell counts were so low that he would struggle to fight off an infection if contracted. Since Jack's skin is so raw and irritated, especially on his belly, they postponed his G-tube surgery. Instead, we were admitted to St. Mary's this evening to have a NG tube (nasal tube) to start nourishing and rebuilding our frail little boy. So the new plan is that we will stay in the hospital for a couple days to get his feedings controlled and build his cell counts back up. Then we will go home, with the NG tube, for a month. We will return in a month and get the G-tube placed, do stem cell harvest and High dose chemo. It definitely is disappointing to not be able to get the G-tube, but as long as he is getting nourishment – we can manage. Good news is that we will probably be home sooner this weekend.

Our celebration for Jack's last day of radiation will have to be delayed, but he will feel better and more willing to celebrate this weekend. Marty and I are so proud of our son. When you hear the radiation doctor explain that they did the maximum radiation and took Jack to the farthest limits they could it hurts, but the overwhelming feelings are for how proud we are of Jack and his victory over the powers of pain. How can we ever NOT achieve a goal in our lives when we see how much our son has achieved! He will forever be our power in life.

God knows that to keep Jack safe, this is our new plan. We look forward to the next month and filling up Jack's "good column".

Thanks, for the prayers and God Bless,

Jen and Marty

The notion of taking Jack home for the first time in over a month was overwhelming. We were excited and scared at the same time. We would be going home, three hours away from our security blanket and the people we had trusted with Jack's life. We checked out of the RMH for the first time in four months. The only time that one of us was not at RMH was when we were on a weekend pass home or at the hospital.

Jack was on a feeding tube because he was not eating by himself. We would run the formula through his NG tube throughout the day and night, taking breaks every so often. It was so frustrating when we would feed him a bag, give him his medicine, and then he would get sick and throw up everything that we had just given him. We would start all over again. This was a very frustrating time for Jack as well. He was home, not as coordinated as before, and he was hooked up to a feeding pole for 12 hours a day. When we would give him a break we tried to let him be a kid again. We would take him outside and he would last 20 to 30 minutes before having to go inside for a nap. You could see determination on his face not to be outdone by Ben and Ella in anything but sometimes he just didn't have it in him and he would become sad. If he could only realize the fight that he was winning he would know that he is very special in his own right.

Journal
Saturday, August 13, 10:42, PM CDT

"Sometimes the great achievements of life are won or lost in the mountains, when the climb is the steepest, when the heart is tested".
-Lance Armstrong

I'm sorry we have not updated for so long. Everything is still going well, we are just crazy busy.

Since the last update:

1.   Jack was feeling so good that he started TAIBO again. Make sure to check out the new pictures. Even Ben is joining in on the exercising!

2.   Jack gained another pound, so he is officially 33 lbs! Jack's blood work continues to remain good.

3.   Papa Tom and Grandma Sis visited on Friday. Unfortunately Jack needed a nap, so grandma was unable to have the WWE playstation rematch. I think she was bummed. Uncle Steve and Aunt Rose also visited. Immediately, Jack found Aunt Rose's lap to be a perfect spot to lay down for a nap. Ben quickly reacquainted himself with Uncle Steve and made him his new playmate. A special thanks to Uncle Steve for entertaining Ben during the visit.

4.   Marty and papa Dan golfed in the "Ed Berger Lymphoma Memorial golf outing" on Friday. Jim Berger (a great friend and deacon that married us) donated ½ of the proceeds to Cancer research and ½ to Jack! Marty really enjoyed himself. Although he wasn't extremely pleased with his game, he did win "closest to the pin." Thanks to the Bergers and all that participated!

5. Friday night Marty, Jack, Ben and I attended the Kernels game. Marty's employer, TrueNorth, had family night at the ballpark. It was our first time "going out" as a family since we have been home. We all had so much fun! It was nice to get to know more of Marty's co-workers, especially since they have been so supportive in the past year. Jack and Ben enjoyed the game and even met Mr. Shucks. On the way out, Jack pleaded to jump in the jumpolene. I decided that he could risk it and "be a kid". The lady that was in charge was very kind to just let Ben and Jack in the jumpolene. I think she even gave them extra minutes. Everyone, right down to the jumpolene lady have been so gracious to us! Thanks to TrueNorth Companies for a fun family night out!

6. On Saturday, we all went to Dyersville for the "Bob Hoeger Memorial Poker Run" which Neil and Linda Hoeger organized on Jack's behalf. Unfortunately it rained, but that did not stop 40 motorcyclists from participating in the charitable event. Thank you to Neil and Linda, as well as all the motorcyclists for braving the weather and doing it for Jack.

7. Ella and I attended a bridal shower for Marty's cousin. Lisa is very special to us, since she babysat the kids a lot when she went to Kirkwood.

She asked if Jack and I would take up gifts at her wedding and we feel quite honored! While Ella and I were at the shower, Marty and the boys were at the cabin enjoying the ol-Miss.

The weekend is not over and we still have fun things planned for tomorrow! We are cramming a summer full of events in one weekend. But, we are bound and determined to enjoy our summer before we go back to MN and reality in less than 2 weeks.

God Bless and Livestrong,
Jen and Marty

Wow, were we living life now! That first night out at the baseball game will stay with me forever. It was the first time in a very long time that I saw Jack be a kid again. He even managed to eat some nachos without getting sick.

We were finding that people were coming out of the woodwork to join in Jack's fight for cancer. It was weekly, and sometimes daily, that we would hear of someone doing something on Jack's behalf. That in itself can be overwhelming.

The quote on the top of that Journal page means a lot to us. Up to this point we really did not know a lot about Lance Armstrong.

Being an avid sports fan, I knew about as much as the average person. I knew who he was and what he did but that was about it. While in the hospital, Jack and I watched Lance go on to win his 6th and 7th Tour de France and I told Jack that Lance had "Spencer" in his body too and that he beat Spencer. Jack began to refer to Lance as the "Livestrong guy." While we were at home I received a package in the mail from our friends Pat and Tracy. In that package was Lance Armstrong's book and audio "It's Not about the Bike." I immediately dove into reading it. It is the most inspirational book that I have ever read. Going through this process with Jack, it was comforting to hear about Lance's story and know his end result because we were so unsure about Jack's. We immediately became Livestrong fans and I made it a goal in my life to try to meet Lance Armstrong and tell him thank you.

Chapter 11
More than God's Power

Journal
Tuesday, August 23, 2005, 9:50 PM CDT

"A delay is not a denial from GOD"

- The Purpose Driven Life

Prior to our ER visit and admittance to the hospital (yesterday), we were visited by Dana (Marty's cousin), Jen, Al, Taylor and 5 other 8-year-old boys. They came to visit and bring toys to Jack and to the Ronald McDonald House Kids. Taylor is an extremely thoughtful 8-year-old boy. For his recent birthday, his parents sent out invitations to the party explaining that the gifts would go to RMH. Taylor and his friends also had a bike wash and did jobs around the neighborhood to earn money for Jack and the RMH. I couldn't express enough how thankful and overwhelmed I was by this young boy's unselfishness and generosity. When Jack met the boys he immediately perked up and smiled. He played games in the RMH gameroom and ate at McDonalds with the big kids. If felt so good to see him be happy and play! Unfortunately the seizures took over and I had to be the bad guy and take him from McDonalds to go to the ER! Hopefully someday he will read this and realize that I would have given anything to have stayed with the boys at McDonalds. Thank-you Dana, Jen, Al and Taylor for the brief but awesome visit.

At the ER, we were blessed by having Nurse Dawn, who listened to me so empathetically. Our insurance should probably be billed for a counseling session, because she made me feel so much better. By 2:00 am we got settled into our hospital room and slept.

Today has been mostly a day of drugs, blood, and calcium and NG feedings. Jack had a reaction to the blood so he needed Benadryl which made him sleep. The doctors are keeping us at the hospital to monitor Jack and get the seizure medicine controlled. Hopefully everything will be controlled in time for the stem cell harvest.

Marty is back and insisted I take some time away from room 136. Lucky for me friends of Marty's from Iowa Realty were in town and offered to take me out for supper. Keith and Theresa provided me a great 2 hour get-away filled with good company and excellent food. I was also able to meet their brother, sister-in law and nephew. They live in Rochester and have also offered to help us in anyway. We continue to be blessed with awesome people.

I have to share one of my newest and best "Jack and Mom moments". Due to seizures and medicine, Jack has been very agitated lately. At times, it is hard to handle, especially since naturally he is a super sweet boy. But before bed Sunday night I told Jack that "I love you so much, I love you bigger than the sky" and he responded "I love you more than God's Power". How can I compete with that one!

We are at the rocky and steep part of the mountain climb, but the neurologist told me that we are ½ way there!

God Bless and Livestrong.
Jen and Marty

More than God's Power! What a powerful statement coming from Jack! Still to this day Jack makes that statement and it blows me away every time. How he ever came up with it we don't know but there is so much about Jack that still amazes us.

The side effects of Jack's seizure medicines were taking over. He would be truly happy one moment and then sad the next. He would fixate on one thing for days, whether it was a toy or a type of food that he wanted. Once you would get it for him he would move on to another thing. It seemed like nothing would keep him satisfied. He would be to the point of being irrational about things and nothing would soothe him. It was so frustrating that Jen and I would take shifts so the other could take a walk to blow off some steam.

Jack would also become very tired at times and be wide awake at others and his sleep habits were totally thrown off. We would take turns staying awake with Jack throughout the night and try to sleep when he slept. Most of the time Jen and I would try to be considerate toward the other but there were times where we just wanted out—out of the hospital room, out of Rochester, and out of this point in our lives.

There was a three-day period when Jack was asleep the entire time. The doctors called this his "radiation hangover" period. He literally was asleep for three entire days. I was with him during this time and would be doing everything imaginable to keep myself busy. I found myself awake around 4:00 a.m. one morning and feeling sorry for myself, I decided that when Jack got better we would talk to the U of I hospitals and share with them the mistakes they had made with Jack's illness. I was feeling very bitter toward the doctors at the U and would not stand still without letting them know of their mistakes. But how would I get it across to them in such a way that it would be positive and they could learn from it and not look at it as a very bitter person pointing the blame? What good could come out of this? So I set to writing an e-mail to Dr. Andrew Lee. He was the one person that helped us to come to the conclusion that a second opinion was needed and for that he is the reason Jack is still alive today. I also copied the two neurologists who were familiar the case on this letter. This is what I wrote to him:

August 30th 2005

Dear Dr. Lee,

I wanted to bring you up to date on my son Jackson Hoeger who you had examined last March.

As you recall you had diagnosed Jackson with pseudotumor cerribri in January. When we came to visit you in March after Jackson was admitted into the hospital from having a long seizure episode you then came to the conclusion that the fluid pressure was gone and that Jackson may have a more serious illness that needed to be addressed.

At that time you had ordered a series of tests to be done, such as another spinal tap and have the pressure measured, another MRI in addition to a MRA and MRV. When we consulted with the neurologist about your request, he stated that he did not want to put Jackson though the risk of sedation to do these tests that he felt were unnecessary. His recommendation was to put Jack on anti-seizure medicine in the hopes that he would grow out of his seizures.

As you would expect, my wife and I were pretty concerned about the difference of opinion between the two of you. Unfortunately for us when we told the neurologist that you had already ordered the tests his response back to us was that you could order them but he had to approve them and he was not going to do that.

With our records in hand we were able to get into the Mayo Clinics in Rochester three weeks later. As you know they reviewed all the records, then wanted to do a series of tests on their own, which included a spinal tap, MRI, MRV, MRA and EEG.

In conclusion Jackson was diagnosed with PNET, which you know is a form of brain cancer. What is special about his form is that there is no mass that has formed. It is a layer of tumor cells that had coated the brain and made its way into the spinal fluid. How they were able to find this was through the series of tests which you had ordered at one time only to be denied. It was through the spinal tap that they got the feeling it was serious. The pressure was so high that it was immeasurable.

My wife and I would like to thank you for your insight on wanting to dive deeper into his illness and not rest on what you thought it was rather find out for sure what it was. It is now the end of August and we have been in Rochester pretty much since the end of March fighting this illness with Jack. We can only think what life would be like for our family had we found this out three weeks earlier and only 20 minutes from our home versus three hours away. He is done with radiation and stem cell harvest and will begin his high dose chemotherapy in two weeks.

Thank you,

Marty Hoeger

After sending this I immediately felt like a weight had been lifted off of my shoulders. Again, our hopes were not to prove anyone wrong rather hope that they were right. I finally felt closure for what had happened at the U of I hospitals. I wondered if I would ever get a response back from him. Well I did. Dr. Lee responded almost immediately to my e-mail by saying:

Dear Mr. and Mrs. Hoeger:

I am so sorry that Jackson is ill but I am glad that a diagnosis was made.

Would it be possible for you to ask Mayo to send us his medical records? This would be most helpful for us here to learn from his case.

Please feel free to contact me at anytime if you have further questions or concerns.

Andrew Lee MD.

Then I received the following from the first Neurologist:

Mr. and Mrs. Hoeger,

Thank you very much for updating us on Jackson. We all benefit from hearing what happens after we see a child. Jackson was very confusing to everyone who took care of him. We will certainly take this opportunity to review his story and learn from it.

I'm very sorry to hear that he has a PNET and you and he have our best wishes.

Thank you again for taking the time to write and sending a copy of your note to Dr. Lee to us.

K. Mathews

I never did receive a response from the second. We later found out that Dr. Lee presented Jack's case to the entire neurology staff at the University of Iowa Hospital. They were at a conference and his entire presentation was about Jackson and his case. He then went on to tell the staff that they had missed the boat on Jack and could have been responsible for his death had his parents not received a second opinion. That's all we wanted—for someone to learn from this and we could not thank Dr. Lee enough.

Journal
Tuesday, August 30, 9:46 PM CDT

Here's a little exercise.

Take your right arm and place it on your left shoulder

Take your left arm and place it on your right shoulder

Now Squeeze

That is the Hoeger family giving all of you a hug.

Thank you for all your prayers and positive vibes...Jack had an MRI today and the doctor gave us the good news that there was considerable change from the MRI taken July 12th. A change for the good.

After the MRI we took Jack back to his room and while placing him on the bed his Hickman tube had pulled apart. We were hopeful that they could fix it rather than replace it which would mean surgery. Ben and I took off for Cedar Rapids. We are an hour away when Jen called us to inform us that it could not be replaced and they will take out the bad one and replace it tomorrow. So we fueled up in New Hampton and headed back up north. The good news is that they are going to place the G-tube in at the same time instead of waiting until Friday. Take the good with the bad and today the good far outweighs the bad.

Again, words cannot express how much we appreciate how much everyone is doing for our family.

So again, THANK YOU!

God Bless and Livestrong

Marty and Jen

Try to imagine going to the doctor's office for the first time and they tell you that they want to check you for cancer and imagine how it would feel leading up to hearing the results. Now, can you imagine knowing you *have* cancer and you go through 38 rounds of radiation on your brain and spine and you're waiting to hear if any of it worked, even a little bit?

Jack had a Hickman line placed into his chest so that they could administer the chemo and stem cells that they were successfully able to harvest the second time. He also had a g-tube placed into his stomach so that we could take out the tube in his nose and administer his drugs and formula through that if needed. The Hickman required changing the dressing every day to prevent infection and the g-tube required cleaning around the hole in his stomach to prevent granular tissue from growing next to it. Jen and I both wanted to be active in these duties so that when it came time to take Jack home we would be confident in our ability to do these things. We also felt that the nursing staff had their hands full and we could relieve them a little bit. And truth be told, we felt we were a little better at it than some of the nurses.

Journal
Monday, September 12, 2005, 8:39 PM CDT

FIRST DAY OF HIGH DOSE CHEMO DONE!

It feels fantastic to say that Jack has been able to begin this toxic treatment that will DESTROY the tumor cells! I am also extremely pleased to report that he had a good day today!

The day began at 8:00 am with the first bag of chemo hung. We followed strict instructions to swab his mouth with a baking soda mixture 4x/day and medicine 2x/day to prevent mouth sores. Jack is not particularly fond of the swabbing, but he is dealing with it. As for nausea, he felt pretty good all day, the swabbing made him sick a couple of times. At 10:00 am the 2nd bag of chemo was hung. This chemo is excuded through his skin, so we have to give him a bath every 4 hours. They will let him sleep from midnight until 6:00 am without waking him for a bath. This regimen will continue tomorrow. Overall, so far so good and very manageable. I guess all of our intense prayers have been heard! We are definitely not out of the woods, but we are very pleased.

I told Jack that this treatment is what is going to beat "Spencer" for good and that God's power and his angels will make him ALL better. Jack told me "I have angels in my head that are beating Spencer." I agreed.

We are starting to see the top of the mountain and feel energized to know that getting there is absolutely obtainable.

Thank you for your prayers and please add our friend Jason to your prayers as he has his MRI on Wednesday!

God Bless you and Livestrong always,

Jen and Marty

When they told us that Jack would receive three rounds of high dose chemo we didn't really know what to expect. How would his body rebound from it? What would the procedure be like? They were about to put the highest dose and most toxic chemical into his body and we felt helpless. All we could do was pray that it worked.

Journal
Sunday, September 18, 2005, 4:55 PM CDT

"Even while resting, the battle inside your body is going on, cell by cell. Sometimes just let the body rest so the cells can concentrate on only one job at a time".

-Quote from the book "There's No Place Like Hope."

The first stem cell transplant was successfully completed! The critical procedure was surprisingly simple. A very important looking person thaws the bags of stem cells and puts them in a syringe for the transplant nurse to slowly inject into Jack. They used 5 bags of stem cells and the procedure lasted approximately 20 minutes. During the transplant, Jack takes on a cream style corn-like odor. He got sick during the transplant because he also got that taste in his mouth. After the transplant, Jack slept for about 3 hours.

After the transplant, the oncologist asked if we wanted go home for the weekend. Shockingly, I said "Home like RMH or Home like HOME-HOME? She laughed and said "Home-Home." She explained that Jack's cell counts wouldn't go down drastically until Monday and to just return then. So I called Marty to tell him to stay in CR and Jack and I headed home! What a great feeling.

Home has made a HUGE difference for Jack. He has found his smile and is happier. He has been able to see his grandparents, his cousins and our neighbors. Home is definitely what the doctor ordered- literally and figuratively!

It is hard not to look at Jack and think about those nasty cells dying. He looks so good for just having gone through the biggest event of his life. But this week is an important week in that his cell counts are going to nearly nothing. We have to pray that his body recovers without contracting a virus or infection. We started the "wonder shots" that will boost his cell production. It is very difficult as a parent to give that shot every day, but it is a necessity. Hopefully he will only need 10 days of it and not any more during transplant.

We were given the best weekend to reenergize and be a family. Ben and Ella have given us the energy we need to proceed. We CAN do this!

Please pray that Jack's cell counts recover without any risks or infection.

Have a great week and Livestrong.
Jen and Marty

We were on pins and needles during this period of Jack's illness. Any little virus could become fatal. We wanted to put Jack into a bubble in the hospital and wait for his cells to rebound. The thought of going home or to the RMH just scared us to death. It would now be up to us to protect him from anything and everything that he would come in contact with.

Our instructions were that if Jack's temperature reached 101 degrees that we were to take him to the emergency room as soon as possible. This would happen on more than on one occasion.

Journal
Friday, September 23, 2005, 7:04 PM CDT

I know that God will not give me something that I cannot handle, I just wish he would not trust me so much".
-Mother Theresa

After a long day yesterday, I was hoping for Jack to have a nice peaceful night sleep. Not so, He continued to become sick throughout the night. He was up every hour from 12:30 to 6:00 asking for a bowl. There were a couple of times that I would awake to him sitting up with the bowl in front of him like he was trying not to wake me.

At 6:00 a.m. I had taken Jacks temperature and it was at 100 degrees. Then at 8:30 it had reached 101, I called the on call doctor and they directed me to the emergency room for some blood work. By the time we made it there his temp had gone back to normal. After some discussion, the decision was made to admit Jack back into the hospital until his counts come back which will be another 4-5 days.

This afternoon his fever returned to 101. Although this was something they had told us might happen, I think that we were holding out a little hope that we were going to luck out and not have to return to the hospital until his next chemo round.

On a positive note, Jack was asking for water today. It was the first time for a couple of weeks that he has shown any interest in putting something in his mouth.

God Bless and Livestrong.

Marty and Jen

What we were experiencing at this point was all of the horror stories of what chemo can do to the body. Jack was so sick and so tired; his body so frail. Jen and I were trying to keep with the system that had worked so well for us for some time now. But with him getting so sick so often it was too much for one person to handle mentally. We decided that for now we all needed to be together.

We were finally discharged from the hospital and told to go home for 10 days until the 2nd round of chemo was to begin. On the way home we noticed that Jack's neck and face started to swell. We reached home around 6:00 p.m. and Jen put a call into the doctors to let them know about the swelling. They asked us to get Jack back into the ER to get it checked out. We didn't even get a chance to unload the van and we were headed north again. We reached the ER at 10:00 p.m. They were stumped; they did scans to the neck and head looking for blood clots. They found nothing. Again Jack had baffled them. After 5 hours of exams they told us to go to the hotel and call the clinic tomorrow.

The next morning we called for our appointment and they informed us that the doctor's instructions were to give him Benadryl and to go home.

The next day Jack came down with a temperature of 101 and we were off to the ER in Cedar Rapids. They discovered that Jack had pneumonia and he was admitted to the hospital in Cedar Rapids with the doctors at St. Mary's calling all the shots. Because he spent most of the day on Friday sleeping, we decided that Jen should take a break and go to my cousin's wedding and I would spend the day with Jack in the hospital. Jack slept for a good part of the morning, then woke up asking for Dad. I would answer him saying, "Jack, I am right here." He would look up at me with his eyes only half open and again, "Dad I want you." I said, "Jack I am right here." He could not see me; his eyes were glossed over and not able to open past mid-line. I called for the doctor and they immediately got Jack's Rochester doctors on the line. The plan was to try to get him comfortable and transport him as soon as possible.

I called Jen and told her to get to the hospital as soon as possible. I thought we were losing him. Was this the cancer finally taking over?

After being transported via ambulance they came to the conclusion that Jack was suffering a seizure and by the time we made it to Rochester he was back to normal. They hooked him up to the EEG monitors to check his seizure activity. The results were astounding. They informed us that Jack was having a seizure sometimes every 2 to 3 seconds. Some were longer and he was experiencing 10 to 20 an hour.

Not only was he physically sick, his brain was in overload fighting these cells.

Journal
Tuesday, November 8, 2005, 7:41 PM CST

Yesterday Jack's platelet counts were up to 71,000!

So within 24 hours we are back in Rochester. Today was long, filled with blood work, hearing test, kidney test, and a doctors appointment. Jack was a trooper, like usual. He even had to get a shot. The hearing test resulted in a high frequency hearing loss in Jack's left ear. He did have some wax in his ear, so we will go back tomorrow to test it again. Hopefully he is able to hear better. We knew loss could occur due to the chemo drugs. In retrospect, a high frequency loss is nothing.

During our oncology appointment we were told that "the team" decided that this would be Jack's last high dose chemo round with stem cell transplant. They are concerned that it took so long for Jack's little body to recover from the last dose and it will only get more difficult. They do not want to destroy his immune system and not be able to build it back up. So Jack will get all of his stem cells back in this last transplant. How do we feel about this? Well we have mixed emotions. We feel like we should be overjoyed that this is the last time that Jack's body will have to endure this awful treatment, yet we feel like we didn't complete the task. The oncologist explained that there is no evidence that 3 doses is any better than 2. We WANT to be done with treatment, but we were just shocked knowing that it is a lot closer than we thought. Maybe we will get our Christmas miracle.

God Bless and Livestrong,
Jen and Marty

Imagine the emotions going through our minds at this point. Remember when we said that we would trust our doctors with Jack's life? It still remained true at this point. The feeling was an uneasy one. This was our last hope. What would we do if it didn't work? We started this fight with a plan, a treatment plan, and now so late in the game it was changing. Our trust in the doctors never waivered, so we didn't even question their decision. The process for his last high-dose chemo had started much like the first and then the stem cell transplant was to follow. Then we had to wait. We were sent home for 30 days to await his first MRI and then to review the results.

We decided to stay in Rochester for a couple of days in case he came down with a fever, which he did within 94 hours of being released. We stayed in Rochester the entire month because Jack would be in and out of the hospital so much. Our Thanksgiving consisted of my cousin Dana and her husband Matt driving down from Minneapolis with a carload of food for us to enjoy in the hospital room. We were extra thankful for them because they saved us from yet one more day of cafeteria food.

Finally his MRI day arrived. He was to get his MRI on Friday morning, then we could go home for the weekend and go over the test results with Dr. Wetmore on Monday.

Chapter 12
Jack the Survivor

Journal

Saturday, December 10, 2005, 3:21 PM CST

AN EARLY SURPRISE...ACCORDING TO OUR NEURO-ONCOLOGIST, THE TUMOR HAS NOT PROGRESSED AND JACK'S SCAN LOOKS A LOT BETTER, THERE ARE A COUPLE SMALL AREAS THAT LIGHT UP, BUT IT COULD BE SCAR TISSUE OR DEAD TUMOR CELLS. OUR DOCTOR WAS PLEASED THAT HE RESPONDED TO THE CHEMO AND WILL SCHEDULE HIM FOR A MRI IN 3 MONTHS. TIME WILL TELL, IF THE BRIGHT AREAS ARE TUMOR CELLS AND IF SO, WE WILL CONTINUE TO TACKLE THIS DISEASE WITH FULL FORCE! OVERALL THE NEWS WAS VERY GOOD!

You are probably wondering how we got the MRI results so quickly. We returned home yesterday, after Jack's MRI, and he seemed to be doing really well. After his bath, Jack became very congested, got the chills and spiked a fever. Marty took Jack to Mercy's ER, where Jack was diagnosed with pneumonia...again. Jack's fever reached 104 degrees and he had trouble breathing. He had seizure after seizure. So at 4:00 am Jack was transported to Mayo via the Mayo jet. Marty and I were unable to go with Jack on the Jet, so we drove north again.

The ride at 4:00 am was scary and exhausting. Poor Marty hadn't slept for over 24 hours and I had a couple of hours of sleep. Except for hitting a sheet of ice while I was driving and fish tailing across the road, we made it safely by 6:45 am.

On the drive, we both feared that Jack beat cancer, but not pneumonia. We were very anxious to get to Mayo and make sure Jack was stable. We were very relieved to see Jack sleeping quietly and maintaining his oxygen with a little help. We were able to get a couple of hours of sleep and meet with the doctor. Besides the great news that Jack is defeating Spencer, he looks better than 12 hours ago. We will stay and get him off of the oxygen tube, and give him IV antibiotics and a platelet transfusion. Our next mission is to beef him up and control these seizures. Fortunately, the doctor doesn't believe the seizures are due to any tumor cells. A crazy, scary, exhausting night has turned out positive. We can't ask for much more than that.

Thank you for the prayers of healing, they continue to work. You have a lot more power than you think.

God Bless and Livestrong.

Jen and Marty

After one light dose of chemo, 38 rounds of radiation, two rounds of high-dose chemo, two stem cell harvests, and rescue procedures and millions of seizures, JACK WAS NOT GOING DOWN TO PNEUMONIA! When I took Jack into the ER that night the doctor looked at Jack's x-rays then looked at me and said we have a very sick boy here. I had given him all of the information from the on-call doctor at Mayo and they came to the conclusion that an ambulance ride was not an option. She informed the staff at Mercy that she was sending down the Mayo jet and they should prepare Jack for transport.

I will never understand why at least one parent cannot ride in the helicopter or airplane with the patient. I remember on one tour of the helicopter hanger in our earlier stays in the hospital that they informed us that that was not an option. I said to myself at the time, "There's no way they would take Jack and not allow me to go with him." Well I am here to tell you that NO means NO! We sent Jack off with the air transport team, many of whom we already knew from our time in the ICU unit, so that made it a little easier.

. . .

Jack was in overtime with his fight. He had done everything that he had been asked to do. He passed every test thrown his way. Now it was time to get healthy and wait.

The months that followed consisted of Jen and me both working part-time and sharing the duties at home with Jack. One of our goals was that we wanted to be home for the holidays as a family. We were able to do that, which made it extra special that year.

Journal
Tuesday, March 21 2006, 4:50 PM CST

"The scan looked better than I ever dreamed it would and I don't get to say that very often!"

-Dr. Cynthia Wetmore, Pediatric Neuro-Oncologist, Mayo.

Now that is the best quote we have written yet on this website! We are still shocked and overwhelmed with emotion!

Marty and I woke up today agreeing that we were just happy that Jack has been seizure-free and the results of the MRI were out of our hands!

Honestly, we were nervous, but calm. Although, I did get a good feeling when Jack picked out two rainbow stickers before his MRI.

Dr. Wetmore was running late for our appointment, but when she walked in she immediately gave us a hug and gave us the awesome news! What a huge relief! Good news for us! She explained that the small bright areas on the last scan were decreased a lot and there were no new enhancements! Basically she could not see any tumor cells! Given that the tumor is an aggressive one, it was a great sign that it did not grow! Granted, the chance of the tumor growing in the first year is still a possibility, however each month the probability decreases! YESSSS!!!!

We were able to schedule getting his Hickman line out next week.

Now we can focus on Disney World and enjoying our next 3 months seizure-free and hopefully Spencer-free!

We are so proud of Jack and feel honored to be his parents. He surprised us and many doctors, many times!! We thank God and all of you for making our miracle happen!

God Bless and Livestrong

Jen and Marty

Finally some tears of joy! Finally we were able to make some plans and feel like they were going to happen.

Jack was fortunate to be selected to go on a Make-A-Wish trip. His wish was to swim with the dolphins and to go to Disney World. Well, with a lot of discussion we finally decided that a Disney Cruise was the way to go with a dolphin excursion thrown in. We went on his trip in May of 2006. It was such a magical trip for all of us. Jack ate more than he had for almost a year. He went swimming, and loved his dolphin experience. We even made a decision not to hook Jack up to the feeding tube one of the days! Between Make-a-Wish and Disney they made us feel like rock stars and helped us put the last year and a half on the back burner for awhile. On our last night of the trip, while getting ready for bed, Ben leaned over to Jack and said, "Good wish, Jack!" Jack just smiled, rolled over, and fell asleep.

Journal
Tuesday, June 20, 2006, 10:18 PM CDT

REMISSION!

We all prayed for the day we could finally hear that one amazing word and today was the day!!

I have to admit, I was nervous today waiting ALL day for our awesome news. But when Dr. Wetmore walked in the door and gave us big hugs, I knew we had great news! She said "It looks good, how's Ollie"? (our 6 month old puppy) We talked about 20 minutes about the dog and Jack's Make-a-Wish trip. I was so relaxed by "its good" but I wanted to know how good. She said that the MRI was clean of any signs of tumor cells and confirmed that Jack was now in FULL REMISSION! Dr. Wetmore reviewed Jack's medical history with us and explained that there is NO treatment protocol for Jack's cancer. When I asked if NOW there would be a report, just in case another child has a diagnosis like Jack…She smiled and nodded gratefully. Maybe this was God's plan for Jack?

We were extremely thankful to say good-bye to Rochester today and actually for the first time in over a year, the town didn't feel like home. What a good feeling! We will live a normal life for the next 3 months and try to not take anything for granted.

May God bless you all twice fold for all the prayers and support you have given Jack and our family during this journey. Jack has finally reached the top of the mountain and we feel it was because you all pulled him over each obstacle he had to overcome! Thank-you!

God Bless and Livestrong.
Jen and Marty

Remission, what a great word, not a word but a state of mind. We left the office that day with a lot more bounce in our step. We finally heard the words that we had prayed for so many times. We finally heard the words that Jack had fought so hard for.

Jack also participated in the Relay for Life that year. On Friday night we attended the lighting of the luminaries. On Saturday morning he did his survivor lap. When it was time for his lap he got into the front of the pack. The walk started out with Jack walking next to Conner and holding our friend Linda's hand. About halfway around the track we could see Conner but we could not see Jack. We then spotted him being carried and passed around by a group of the survivors. This was so emotional for us; Jack had come so far but seeing this made us realize just how far he still had to go. Coming down the stretch his face lit up, he was smiling from ear to ear. He looked at me as I took him from one of the survivor's arms and he said, "Dad I did it!" You sure did, Jack! A survivor lap!

Our next mission was to put some meat on his bones and get him ready for school coming up in the fall. That was something that we weren't sure was ever going to happen.

Journal
Monday, July 31, 2006, 7:33 AM CDT

One survivor meets another!

Last Friday Jen and I escorted Jack to his first Senate hearing. The purpose of this hearing was to discuss the topic of cancer awareness and the 40 million dollar budget cuts made to the cancer research fund.

Speaking at the hearing was Senator Tom Harkin, Senator John Kerry, a U of I doctor, a cancer survivor, a cancer volunteer for 30 years and Lance Armstrong. After the hearing we took Jack up to the stage to see if he could meet Lance. As soon as we reached the stage we saw that the entire panel had already left the room. So we decided to have some fun on the stage. While letting Jack do his thing on stage a lady informed us that Lance would be more than happy to see a couple of kids that were still around. We were off, a small parade of children with some parents headed off down the hall to see Lance.

He was very accommodating to the kids. He spoke with them, signed autographs, and took several pictures. It was great to finally meet this icon that had given so much of his life to the cause of curing cancer.

Jack is doing great, this weekend was pretty laid back, enjoying the confines of our air conditioning. Sunday Jen took the boys to the store to purchase school supplies. What a difference a year makes. Last year at this time we were watching Jack in the fight of his life on a day to day basis. Now he is getting ready for school.

Thank you for your prayers and support.

God Bless and Livestrong!
Marty and Jen

Jen, Jack, and I were at the Senate hearing—all of us dressed in our Livestrong shirts. We wanted everyone there to understand what it is like to "Livestrong" because Jack had done it and still is doing it to this day. When we were back in Lance's green room it was the moment that I had thought about for a long time. I had always wondered what I would say to him if I ever had the chance to meet him. Well now it was time. What words of wisdom could I share with him about Jack's journey? I stood with him face to face and said, "Thank you." That's it, just thank you. He looked at me and then to Jack and the look on his face was that he understood and that's all that needed to be said. He signed a Livestrong jersey that we had and hung out with us for 15 minutes. A moment to be cherished forever.

Chapter 13
Miracles DO Happen!

Journal
Tuesday, November 28, 2006, 7:50 PM CST

"It's a miracle!"

-Dr. Cynthia Wetmore, Pediatric NeuroOncologist

Jack is officially cancer-free for a year!! Dr. Wetmore gave us a big hug and couldn't believe how good Jack looked. She said the scan remains clean of cancer cells and expects Jack's brain to continue to heal in the next year. She said "It's a miracle!" With each scan she is more honest about her feelings and concerns during Jack's treatment. She was so optimistic during Jack's treatment, but deep down was very scared for him. We all prayed for a miracle, but until your doctor tells you it was a miracle, you can't believe it!

She was very pleased with everything that Jack has been doing to get strong again. She wants Jack to gain more weight, so we will try an appetite stimulant again. Other than that, we will see her again in 3 months and keep livingstrong!

During our visit, Dr. Wetmore complimented Marty and I on how well we managed during Jack's treatment. She said we should write a book because it could help so many other families that have kids diagnosed with brain cancer. She took me by surprise and I asked "Have you been reading our website?" So signs are everywhere, we just need to be open for them.

We prayed for a Christmas miracle last year and have been blessed again with yet another miracle! It just shows you how prayers, faith and hope can cause miracles!

THANK-YOU for your prayers, we would not be so strong without you!

God Bless and LIVESTRONG,
Jen and Marty

It's a miracle! When Dr. Wetmore said those words everything started to sink in. Jack's form of cancer had never had a treatment plan before and now they had one. She once told me that she was not there to be our cheerleader, she was there to save Jack's life, and she did. The entire team had. Dr. Rodriguez, Dr. Arndt, Dr. Kahn, Dr.

Andy, Dr. Erin, Dr. Kotagal Julia, Holly, Warren, all of the nursing staff at St. Mary's third floor pediatric unit, the radiation "Dream Team," Dr. Kumar, Dr. Lee, the entire third floor pediatric ICU unit nursing staff, Elaine and the child life staff, everyone at the Ronald McDonald House, The Make-A-Wish Foundation—it's a miracle that you all came into our lives to save Jack's life.

It's a miracle that we have been blessed with so many friends and family members who were there at a moment's notice. We have been blessed to have a church community that has kept us close to their hearts and prayers. We have been blessed to have employers who would be right there with us, no questions asked. "Just take care of Jack and your family and come back to work when its time," was their comment to us every time we showed up to work and they knew we were at a different place mentally.

People ask us how we do it? How do we live life with cancer? To be honest with you I cannot imagine life without it. It seems so long ago. Life with cancer is hell, no doubt about it, but when you see that Jack has taken every battle that presented itself head on and won . . . It's a miracle!

Most of all it's a miracle to have been blessed with a son who refuses to give up. Even when his parents wanted to give up so many times, he would show us that giving up was not an option. Never give up hope because even in the darkest of valleys there's always a path to the top of the mountain. You just have to have hope.

Jen and I have dreams and visions of how we can give back. We have always told Dr. Wetmore that if we were ever to come into money, her cancer research would be at the top of our list. Her answer was one that hit us like a ton of bricks. She said, "There are plenty of people who can give money, you guys have knowledge. You can give your gift in words." Well, since we have a lot more words than money—here is our small gift back.

God Bless and LIVESTRONG!

Marty and Jen

Epilogue

Jennifer L Hoeger

For some reason, we had the notion that once Jack was done with his chemotherapy, life would be the same again…or at least easier. What we didn't' expect was that it would take Jack almost as much strength to build himself back up as it did to fight cancer.

The first 3 months after Jack's treatment were very hard. It was wonderful to be home and have completed the treatment, but it was just as scary not getting the treatment also. Basically it was a waiting game to see if the treatment worked. To not get chemo, meant we were not fighting cancer anymore. At least when he was being transfused with toxic chemicals we felt that we were actively saving his life. Now we just had to wait for 3 months until the next MRI and see if the treatment worked.

At that time, Jack didn't appear free of cancer. He didn't even look healthy. Jack continued to suffer from "drop seizures." He would literally just drop. It seemed to never fail, that if he was sitting at the kitchen table, he would have a seizure and slam his head on the table. If he was standing up, he would just collapse. They were quick, but strong seizures. He would often scream or cry after each one, then fall asleep. There were times he would have more than 20 a day. He had very little quality of life at that time and we were worried that it was a sign that the cancer was not gone.

Jack was mostly sedentary because of seizures, being hooked up to the feeding tube and just being sick. He had very little muscle left to support his frail body. He was so weak he could not even support himself to sit on the toilet. When he did try to play, he was constantly spraining his ankles. It took over 3 months, but the neurologist found the right cocktail of seizure medicines to control the drop seizures. We started to see glimpses of the old Jack returning. He started having more energy so we started physical and occupational therapy. It was time to begin the rebuilding of Jack.

Since Jack was on so much medicine, up to 7 seizure medicines at a time, Jack had a very little appetite. Jack used a gastric feeding tube to keep him hydrated and gain weight. The tube was bitter sweet. It took the stress away from knowing if Jack was getting nutrition, however he tended to aspirate his tube feedings. Like a predictable cycle, Jack would get pneumonia, spike a fever, go into the hospital, get antibiotics, get diarrhea from the antibiotics, and lose all the weight he had gained. It was also a constant balance of the right amount of feeding to not make him sick.

To help Jack gain weight, our oncologist prescribed "Marinol." Marinol is a drug with the active ingredient in marijuana. The marinol was suppose give Jack the munchies and help him gain weight. Apparently, it is not prescribed much to our pharmacy, because I was semi-interrogated over the drive-thru loud speaker. They asked if I knew what was prescribed with a suspicious look on their face. I said, "Yeah, marijuana to stimulate my son's appetite." The pharmacist kept looking at me like, "really, for your son?" I said, "I'm not looking to get the munchies and gain weight!" Marinol worked at first, but he became tolerant of it and needed more to become hungry. However the more we gave him, the more loopy he would become.

The stress of getting Jack to eat was endless. If something sounded good to him, we would get it for him. Most of the time, he would be lucky to take a bite of whatever we bought him. I bet we spent over a thousand dollars on food that he thought he would eat, just for him to not even be able to take a bite. When the marijuana drug kicked in, Jack would get hooked on a specific food and that is all he would eat. There were phases of spaghettios, Zio Johnos garlic bread, Chinese food, peanut butter sandwiches and fudge dipped granola bars to name a few. If we were somewhere without the specific food, a substitute would not do. We would plead, bribe and out of frustration yell to try to get him to take a bite. It was heart breaking to hear at doctor appointment's that Jack had "failure to thrive" or that he was "malnourished." Everyday we struggled to get food into him and keep it in him. It would not be until February of 2008 until the gastric tube was finally removed.

After treatment, we waited for Jack's brain to heal. Jack's doctors were unsure of how much his damaged brain would heal. We weren't sure who Jack was anymore. Was he agitated all the time because of the medicine or brain damage? Jack had so many variables to try to understand him. He had seizures, brain damage, and so many side affects to medicine that you wonder if taking the medicine was worth it. After one MRI, the doctor told us that Jack's brain was continuing to have atrophy. Basically, Jack's brain was getting smaller due to the affects of radiation from a year previously. That hit us hard. I kept thinking, "What do you mean his brain is getting smaller, he is supposed to be getting better by now!" We were constantly reminded by the doctors that they didn't know exactly what to expect because there was no one like Jack. That was for sure!

One thing that never changed was Jack's loving disposition. When he sat by you, you meaning ANYONE, he was on your lap or holding your hand. Jack was with at least one of us 24/7. So when he slept by me, he always held my hand. When he felt good, he hugged everyone. He was always what I called a "smoozer," just ask his preschool teachers. So when I became sad that he had lost so many skills that were once so easy for him, I would thank God that he was still a "smoozer."

We knew that Jack would have some learning difficulties, but we were not prepared for how much he would struggle mentally due to cancer. Since Jack's brain cancer covered the entire cortex, there wasn't an area that was not affected. The cancer affected his vision, perception, writing, auditory processing, memory, problem solving, and social skills. I would like to think that I wasn't a person in denial and naturally I was more aware of Jack's cognitive skills due to my profession, but I was wrong.

We were thrilled when Jack was strong enough to attend kindergarten the fall of 2006 at Jackson Elementary. He was only able to manage half days for a couple months as he was still on a lot of seizure medicines and still pretty frail. It was not until Jack started attending school, did I realize the impact of his treatment for him cognitively. He struggled even following simple directions. It broke our hearts to see him struggle to write a letter and not retain it. Jack would work so hard and not retain much. The school quickly called a meeting with us to discuss how to best serve Jack. It was then that I fell a part, unfortunately in front of a large table of people I didn't know. I felt like a failure as a mom and as a speech pathologist as I confessed that I didn't know Jack would struggle that much. In actuality, we didn't know who Jack was now. We didn't know if it were side effects of all the medicine or the brain damage that caused Jack his challenges. Those people around that large table quickly set up a plan for Jack and were able to get Jack an aid to assist him. That day we no longer felt alone in

Jack's rebuilding process. Little did we know that those people and the entire staff and student body of Jackson Elementary would become our rock of support for Jack in a way we did not expect.

Jack's kindergarten teacher, Mrs. Reid, welcomed him with a huge hug and continues that tradition everyday at school since. She is a true angel that we are blessed to have in our lives. It took a special teacher and aid to manage Jack's kindergarten year of roller coaster good health and sickness. That December Jack developed another kind of seizure. Every morning about an hour after he woke up he would go into a seizure where he would nod his head and move repetitively. He would have it for up to nearly 5 minutes. Then fall asleep due to the exhaustion from the seizure. It would happen again about at 8:00 at night. How do send your child to school to learn after that? How do you expect him to learn? What do you expect? We spent several days at Mayo clinic doing a video seizure study. Eventually, we were told that Jack was experiencing a type of seizure that were the most difficult to control. We were told by one doctor that Jack would never drive a car or be independent at most activities. Our neurologist was upset by the negative, but factual information we were given. Instead of giving up on Jack, he suggested an experimental treatment for the debilitating seizures. We were not failed by this wonderful man yet, so upon his prescription we started Jack on ACTH shots. Traditionally, the injections are used for infantile seizures, but were not trialed on kids Jack's age or for this sort of seizure. After about 6 weeks of the injections, the seizures were controlled. For the first time in over a year, Jack was hungry again! The injection was form of steroid and boosted Jack's appetite. We felt like Jack was finally going forward again.

By May of Jack's kindergarten year, he was getting stronger physically and working hard mentally. We were ready to show the world that Jack beat cancer and we were determined to increase cancer awareness and raise money for a cure. With the wonderful energy of Mrs. Reid and the entire Jackson school, we had our first LIVESTRONG Day event on May 17th. Our mission was to raise awareness and money for the LIVESTRONG Foundation and the American Cancer Society Relay for Life. Thanks to the kindergarten parents and Mrs. Reid, every Friday for the month we had a bake sale to raise money. The Jackson elementary raised over $500.00 in selling $.25 baked goods! Not to mention nearly the entire school bought yellow "Team JACKSTRONG" shirts to wear on LIVESTRONG Day. That day the entire school wearing their sea of yellow shirts walked around the school trail to support and honor those with cancer. It was a great beginning to educating our kids about cancer and inspire them to help find a cure.

Also that May, I was honored to be selected to be an Iowa delegate for the Lance Armstrong Foundation to go to Washington D.C., on LIVESTRONG Day to lobby for more cancer funding. Those couple days changed my life and it all began before I even left the Cedar Rapids airport. Prior to leaving on my trip, I prayed for guidance and to have the right words to inspire our elected officials and anyone I came into contact. I knew I was given an incredible opportunity to make a difference and I knew I needed some divine intervention. The day before I left for capital hill, which happen to be Mother's day, the local news interviewed me about Jack and going to Washington D.C.. The next morning at the airport waiting for my plane, several strangers in the terminal recognized me from the news and we got talking about my trip and Jack. An elderly couple overheard me and wanted to know more about Jack. I showed them a picture and explained the rare brain tumor story. The 80 year old man had tears running down his face. Now, by then I was use to the gracious tears people had for Jack, but I wasn't expecting what happened next. The elderly wife reached into her wallet and handed me a picture of a boy about 8 years old. She explained that it was her grandson that died many years ago because of brain tumor just like the one I explained that Jack had. I couldn't believe it. I just met the grandparents of a child who is one of less than 12 ever diagnosed with Jack's cancer. We shared tears, laughs and how cancer changed our lives. I gave them Jack's picture and know that they hold in there hearts our meeting as dear to them as I do. I am telling you, there are no coincidences!

My trip to Capitol Hill was amazing with lifelong friendships made. I learned how to "make the ask," which would later change our lives. Lance Armstrong's story had importance in our life, but now the foundation had become just as important. I was educated on how to build a local army and succeed in a grass roots effort to fight cancer. I had the passion, now I was given the tools. I handed each elected official and anyone who would listen a picture of Jack in a Spiderman costume that read "With great power comes great responsibility." I was determined to spread Jack's story to hopefully inspire and make a difference.

As I was becoming the political advocate with the Lance Armstrong Foundation, Marty was selected by the Foundation to ride in the Registered Annual Bike Ride Across Iowa (RAGBRAI) for Team LIVESTRONG. Marty raised money to ride with the team and raise awareness throughout the entire state of Iowa. Marty made lasting friendships from people all over the world. He was responsible with his teammates to help raise over $300,000 to support those with cancer. We felt blessed to have our outlets to give back and to honor Jack's fight.

As Jack was on the road to more recovery than sickness, we tried to shift more towards concentrating on the positives of cancer versus the negatives. As Marty explained earlier in the book, we were supported and lifted up by our family, friends and hundreds of strangers. We accepted money and help. In order to do this and not feel saddened by the need, we vowed to give back. Not only were we passionate about the Lance Armstrong Foundation, but we were grateful for our local American Cancer Society.

A little over a year from being diagnosed, we attended our first American Cancer Society (ACS) Relay for Life in Cedar Rapids, Iowa.

We were not sure what to expect. We didn't know very many people that went. But what we did know, was that there was a survivor lap and we wanted Jack to be among the survivors walking. The Relay for Life has teams of people that raise money and walk from Friday evening until Saturday morning with the survivor lap closing the relay. Fortunately, we met up with an old family friend who was a breast cancer survivor. She took Jack with her to do the survivor lap. It was an emotional lap around a track with cancer survivors wearing their ribbons showing the years of remission. There were maybe 5 kids in total. Jack was too weak to walk even 100 yards of the walk, so 3 breast cancer survivors took turns carrying Jack the rest of the lap. That powerful image of those strong woman carrying Jack still makes me cry. At that very moment, Team Jack strong was born and would be one more way for us to try to fight cancer.

In March of 2007, Marty and I were brainstorming about how we would raise awareness and money for Team LIVESTRONG and the Relay for Life. I remembered what I learned from the LAF the year prior about "making the ask." We had just lost our dear friend, Jason Hill, to cancer that February and because of him I was even more determined to raise awareness. I had an idea to have Jack make a short video and send it to our friends in hopes they would pass it along and help raise awareness. I thought if we did it right, people would also donate to our cause. Shortly after my idea, the LAF had a contest to make a video and put it on youtube. The contest helped me get the video done as there was a deadline. It also gave me the use of a song I wanted to use. The only thing was, we had no clue what youtube was about and we could barely download music on our ipod. So we made the ask! Our great friend Bryce was a college friend of ours that we hadn't seen forever. He was a partner in a successful media company. He is a very busy man, but accepted to do us this huge favor. Mind you, he played in a band the night before into the late hours and had an awful sinus infection. We only expected him to download some pictures and music and maybe video tape Jack a little. AGAIN, what we didn't expect was 8 hours of meticulous work to make an incredible, professional video. He was also the brains behind the key phrase "I KNOW JACK!" The video was on youtube that Saturday night. Bryce, Marty and I sent out emails to every person in our address book asking them to please watch the video and pass it along. Our goal was 10,000 views by LIVESTRONG Day, which was in over month. Well we underestimated our family and friends because we had 10,000 in 2 days! The news interviewed us about the video and aired 90% of it several times in the days following. People all over the world were posting comments and emailing us. I sent the video to the LAF making the deadline for the contest that day. We were notified that Jack's video won and his video was put on Lance's blog! From then on, we have sold almost 2000 t-shirts saying "If you don't fight cancer, you don't know Jack!" with "I KNOW JACK" on the back. People all over helped us fundraise because they saw the video. The LAF asked me to help lead a group at the Lance Armstrong Summit in Ohio in July 2008. The LAF showed Jack's video and 1,000 people stood up and chanted "I KNOW JACK" after I introduced myself as "Jack's mom." All of this because we made the ask! Please go to www.youtube.com/livestrongjack to view the video. I'm making the ask again, please pass along the video so we can reach even more people.

Jack's cancer may be gone, but we all feel the affects of it. Marty and I have spoke mostly about Jack, but we have two other children that we love just as much. Ben and Ella have not escaped from the rippling affects of cancer. Ella had just turned one when Jack started showing signs of being sick. Ben was not even three years old yet. For almost 9 straight months, Ben and Ella lived with Grandpa Dan and Grandma Rosie. They made trips on the weekend to stay with my sister, Amy and her family. When we went to Mayo, Ella was barely talking and by the time we were home she was speaking in sentences. I prayed hard that God would spare Jack physical scars and Ben and Ella emotional scars.

I tell Ben, "God gave us you because we needed you." Ben always seemed like a man in a little boy's body. He was always independent, even from a very young age. For instance, on Christmas Eve night when Ben was 10 months old, Marty and I were getting supper ready and we looked over and Ben walked across the floor. That is how Ben learned to walk. Not by coaxing him with our arms open, he just did it. Ben just seemed to always know what to do. He was wiser than his age. But we didn't realize that he would have to become wiser than he should at the young age of 3.

Instinctly, Ben would grab the "puke bowl" for Jack when he heard him coughing. When I took a 5 minute shower, Ben would keep me posted if Jack was having a seizure or not. By 3 years old, Ben knew about hospitals, seizures, radiation, chemo, and feeding tubes. Ben not only was the key to our survival, but he provided the energy and comic relief we needed to keep going. He was also the key to Ella's security. Ben was the one constant in her little life.

Ben speaks about time as "before Jack was sick" and "after Jack was sick." Even though Ben is a wise boy, he still has been hurt by the chaos of cancer. It still makes me sad that we missed Ben's 4-year-old preschool Christmas program because Jack was admitted to St. Mary's hospital due to seizures. Thank-you to our great friend, Shelley, she made a DVD of the program. What we didn't know is that Ben kept a secret from us. He was Santa Claus in the program. At the end of the program, he looks up in the balcony and waves to the video camera and says "Merry Christmas." Ben was very sad we weren't there, but he never cried. He seemed to try to spare our feelings. I can't wait to see what he becomes when gets older, he sure has made a difference to us already.

As for Ella, she has always known Jack to be sick. As early as she can remember, she was sitting on my lap as Jack got blood transfusions. She held his hand when he got his blood taken. She ran to get him tissues for his constant runny nose. Ella understands Jack sometimes better than all of us. She just knows him, not who he was, but just who he is now.

Occasionally, our friends and family will call Marty and I to give advice about how to cope with cancer. We still don't feel equipped with all the answers. I can tell you what I have learned to the key of coping … is being grateful. It sounds strange and I feel funny telling people that because most the time you want to say "this sucks" or "this isn't fair!" Believe me, sometimes it feels good saying that also, just as long as you get to the point of being grateful. To keep from crying incessantly, I made up the "15 minute rule." When you live in a small hospital room, you have no where to go to be alone with your feelings. So I cried in the shower a lot. It was a private spot where hopefully the water drowned out the noise of my sobbing. I devised the "15 minute rule," because there were days I didn't know if I could stop. The rule was based on allowing me to cry for 15 minutes and allowing 5 minutes after that if I needed, but after that I had to reorganize myself to be positive. I found that if you don't get to the point of gratefulness, the negative effects of your battle sucks you in and keeps you there. The reality of Jack's struggles is a lot to handle many days, and what gets us through the day sometimes is being grateful he can just give us a hug.

CPSIA information can be obtained at www.ICGtesting.com
Printed in the USA
LVOW080023271012

304652LV00001B/69/P